"LEADERSHIP AND MANAGEMENT IN A VUCA BUSINESS ENVIRONMENT"

José Bolton Sr., Ph.D.

"LEADERSHIP AND MANAGEMENT IN A VUCA BUSINESS ENVIRONMENT"

"Management is efficiency in climbing the ladder of success; leadership determines whether the ladder is leaning against the right wall."
— *Stephen Covey*

Copyright © 2025 All Rights Reserved

Dedication

This work is dedicated to the courageous men and women who, throughout history, have fought valiantly to bring about positive change for all of humanity. In the spirit of the African proverb, "It takes a village to raise a child," this tradition has fostered a global village and bestowed a legacy of positive human relations to emulate. I am deeply honored to have served alongside those remarkable individuals, both in and out of uniform. I proudly salute those who made it possible for others to build on their legacy. They shaped this nation, giving their hearts, bodies, and souls to uphold our core values and improve the world.

Acknowledgments

I thank my parents, Claude M. Bolton Sr. and Annie Lee Bolton, for allowing my brothers and sisters and me to start our lives in a welcoming community. We were all inculcated with the values of God, Country, and Family.

I thank the federal employees, military personnel, and civilians for their selfless service and mentorship. I also thank my siblings, Claude Junior, Mary, Amelia, Easley, and Thomas, for their unique ways of inspiring responsibility and ethics. I owe a significant debt of appreciation to my family, including my wife, Carol; sons, Jose Junior and Jeffery J.; daughter-in-law, Christina; and grandsons, J and Wentworth: many thanks and all my love to each of them.

About the Author

José Bolton, Sr., Ph.D., has earned national and international recognition as a Human Resources facilitator, an Innovation and Inclusion consultant, a Dean of EO/EEO Education, and an executive consultant. Dr. Bolton has been on the academic staff of the Air Force Academy, Chapman University, University of Maryland, University of Phoenix, Air Force Institute of Technology, Defense Equal Opportunity Management Institute, Father Flanagan's Boys Town National Resource and Training Center, and CEO of 3Bs Executive Consulting.

The reader might find these books of interest too:

1. *The 5 Critical Shades Of Inclusion And Innovation*
2. *Melanie & Her Friends Make A Difference*
3. *Leading An Inclusive And Innovative Organization*
4. *Innovation By Design: The CEO's Manual For Inclusive Leadership*
5. *Leading Inclusion: An Innovative Approach To DEI*

Preface

This book serves as a guide for CEOs, focusing on the complexities of leadership and management within a VUCA (Volatility, Uncertainty, Complexity and Ambiguity) environment. It aims to help CEOs understand and tackle leadership and management challenges in a rapidly changing business landscape. It is specifically designed for new CEOs, leaders, and managers seeking to enhance their skills in a challenging environment by previewing the work of a select group of influential authors and thinkers, who illustrate key leadership principles. It emphasizes the importance of knowledge in these areas and highlights the crucial role it plays in effective decision-making, employee engagement, and organizational resilience. Ultimately, it highlights the importance of ongoing learning and development in adapting to the rapidly evolving business environment. The author attempts to integrate leadership and management thinking in a discussion of how these two underpinnings of successful enterprises worldwide can battle the VUCA environment with timely strategies.

Contents

Dedication 2

Acknowledgments 3

About the Author 4

Preface 5

Introduction 10

PART I: Leadership 14

Chapter 1 Leadership, My Kingdom For Leadership 16

    What is Leadership? 16

    Leadership Lessons 17

    Five Critical Strategies That Build Leaders 23

Chapter 2 The Leadership Mysteries Enigma 28

    Thirteen Well-known leaders and their styles: 28

    Ineffective Leaders 34

    The Effective Leaders Know Themselves 39

    The MBTI personality types are listed below 42

    The Ideal Team Player and His Virtues 47

    Effective Communication 48

    Empathy in Communication 50

Chapter 3 Developing Innovative and Inclusive Leadership Competencies 52

    Reinforcing strategies 52

    Implementing these strategies 55

    Critical Elements of Leadership Mastery 60

    Leadership Development 61

    Preparing to Lead an Inclusive Organization.. 62

Chapter 4 Critical Thinking 64

    A Critical mode of thinking 65

    Tools of Critical Thinking.. 65

    Gathering Facts.. 67

    Reaching Conclusions using Logic 71

    Micro-Aggressions 74

Chapter 5 Role of I&I Professionals in Facilitating Change................ 76

    Understanding I&I Professionals.. 76

    Value Proposition of I&I Professionals 77

    Building Effective I&I Strategies 79

    Change Management... 80

    Ways to Ensure Effective Change Management................................ 82

    Engaging and Empowering I&I Professionals...................................... 82

    I&I Professionals as Change Agents.. 83

Part II Multiple Management Perspectives 86

Chapter 6 Understanding Power Dynamics and Privilege................. 87

    Power Dynamics in Organizations... 88

    Understanding Privilege.. 88

    The Adverse Impact Of Power Imbalance 89

    Tips and Tricks for Navigating Power Dynamics................................ 90

- Building a More Equitable Workplace 92
- Impact of power dynamics and privilege in workplaces 93
- Case Study — Marc Benioff, Salesforce 93
- Conclusion 94

Chapter 7 Engaging Employee Resource Groups (ERGs) and Allies 95
- Difference between ERG and BRG 99

Part III Dynamic Business Environment..100

Chapter 8 Culture..101
- Organizational Cultures and Values 103
- Corporate culture: Is it the same as organizational culture? 105
- The modeling period 108
- Cultural Beliefs 111
- Cultural Intelligence (CQ) 113
- CQ Drive..113
- Organizational And Social Cultures Are Transmitted From Generation To Generation. 119

Chapter 9 VUCA - The Nature of Our World....................................120
- VUCA and Its Nature..120
- Fundamentals of VUCA 121
- A VUCA situation..123
- VUCA and I & I...124
- A VUCA situation can 126
- Collaboration by Leaders and Managers 130
- Benefits of Discussing VUCA Elements 130

    Implications for Leadership And Management 131

Chapter 10 Leadership and Management Strategies 133

    Executive Coach 134

    An Agency Coaching Program Outline 135

    Who and what roles should you consider for executive coaching support after yourself? 137

    Organization Assessment 139

    An Organizational Climate Assessment Outline 139

    Other factors to be considered in coaching 145

    Change Management 146

    Significant Barriers To Change: 148

    A Simple Process For Change Is A Necessity. 148

    The PDAS Procedure 148

    Tailored Strategies For Change. 149

Chapter 11 The End and The Beginning* 150

Chapter Summaries 155

Leadership And Management Strategies 163

Appendix A END NOTES 168

Introduction

You are stepping into a role that demands strategic vision, agility, the ability to lead a diverse and, potentially, international team across multiple functional departments, and manage a talented and effective workforce in a rapidly changing business environment. If that is you and that is the environment you will work in, this book is for you. Take this book with you as you navigate the complexities of leadership, management, and the VUCA (Volatility, Uncertainty, Complexity and Ambiguity) business environment.

This same perspective helped my thinking and solidified my philosophy and outlook as an executive and later as an executive coach. The organization I was working for had created a program to ensure that its leaders, as well as those it termed "high-potential" executives, were prepared to lead and manage multi-million-dollar operations. In the spring of 2009, I was initiating the first session of executive coaching with executives who were onboarding or taking on a new position. Indeed, the budget was critical, but far more important were the 500,000 employees who worked in numerous locations worldwide.

All of them had worked for this organization for decades. They were leaders and managers who had worked on the most demanding and exciting projects for years. They were loyal, diligent, and would die for the organization's goals. They were an inclusive and innovative collection of professionals. They had all worked hard and made sacrifices to be where they were and, more importantly, where the company wanted them. In opening the session, I correctly anticipated their very relevant questions. What will it take to be successful? Where can I go for answers to my questions? What are the real challenges? What can get me into trouble?

What could I share about leadership and management that they didn't already know? In fact, in the world in which they worked, they were truly successful and the envy of their peers. They were ready and confident that they could address any challenge; they were the experts. But what were their keys to success? What guide did their supervisor use to determine which employee had the "Right Stuff" to continue leading the organization?

According to Marshall Goldsmith's 2007 book *"What Got You Here Won't Get You There,* **"The trouble with success is that we often learn how our previous success can prevent us from achieving even more success."**

Goldsmith uses the Kiosk at the mall entrance to illustrate his observation. That kiosk allows us to see the "big picture" as we find ourselves on the big map and thus come to a conclusion about the shortest route to take to the store we want to visit. We examine it to determine our current location and the location of our target store or office within the mall. It usually works, and most importantly, it saves us time. But others may use the "dead reckoning" approach. They continue moving ahead until they find the correct store. Losing time, being distracted, and often exhausted.

One thing is essential: these two approaches are common to all of us and, at one time or another, seem to explain how we made decisions and determined our next steps. Are they the same techniques? Can you use either one at any time? Could you effectively run an organization using these approaches?

A few people never need a kiosk, and instead, they forge ahead blindly. They're blessed with an internal compass that orients them automatically. They always make the correct turn and end up where they intended by the most economical route.

> **Some people go through life with this unerring sense of direction. It guides them not only in shopping malls but in their school years, careers, marriages, and friendships. When we meet people like this, we say they're grounded. They know who they are and where they're going. We feel secure around them. We feel that any**

surprises will only be pleasant surprises. They are our role models and heroes. Marshall Goldsmith, 2007

One of the attendees in this open onboarding session spoke up to say, *"dead reckoning"* was a phrase he heard his spouse use, and it frequently led them to dead-end parking lots. NO!!! Neither of these will work exclusively. This book will take us into another zone. All the news is good news, but one must remember there will always be new news and new opportunities.

This book will discuss this changing environment and how CEOs must prepare for it by enhancing their leadership and management skills. Leadership that is visionary, principled, transformational, and anticipatory. Management that is collaborative, innovative, inclusive, resilient, and focused on goal measurements. These essential skills enable them to possess the agility they need to navigate the Volatility, Uncertainty, Complexity, and Ambiguity of the dynamic world in which we live. Witness the moment these four elements suddenly emerged during the worldwide devastation of the cost of living resulting from new, explosive tariffs and unrelenting wars.

In today's rapidly changing business environment, leaders and managers face unprecedented challenges that require agility, resilience, and strategic foresight. The concept of VUCA—Volatile, Uncertain, Complex, and Ambiguous—captures the essence of these challenges, highlighting the need for adaptive leadership and effective management.

PART I: Leadership

Chapter 1
Leadership,
My Kingdom For Leadership

We've found that 40 percent of executives hired at the senior level are pushed out, fail, or quit within 18 months. This is expensive in terms of lost revenue, costly in terms of hiring individuals, and damaging to morale.

Kevin Kelley, 2009

Thousands of books have been written on the topic of leadership. At one point, it was noted that over 64,000 books were published on this subject. Many of these books specifically address the efforts of the world's leaders. These leaders are so well-known throughout history that even schoolchildren can recognize their names and recall the events that made them so memorable. (See Appendix A)

What is Leadership?

Leadership is often defined by critical, high-stakes decisions, such as those made in wartime, as seen in the lead-up to D-Day. On Dec. 19, 1944, Eisenhower, British Air Marshal A. W. Tedder, and other "D-Day Inc." executives met with Gens. Omar Bradley and Patton. Ike, according to his book *Crusade in Europe*, began the conference by saying, "The present situation is to be regarded as one of opportunity for us and not of disaster. There will be only cheerful faces at this conference table." Michael Korda described the reaction in his book *Ike: An American Hero*: "Patton, who grasped Ike's strategy intuitively, smiled broadly and said, 'Hell, let's have the guts to let the sons of bitches go all the way to Paris, then we'll cut 'em off and chew 'em up.'"

Leadership Lessons

7 Leadership Lessons from a Battle of the Bulge Veteran, 101st Airborne Division Paratrooper

"At 96 years of age, Dr. Frank Tangherlini is still a busy man with the energy and memory of someone half his age. After getting his PhD from Stanford, he became a renowned theoretical [physicist](#) who even has a physics concept named after him.
But in December 1944, Frank Tangherlini was just another 20-year-old US Army Private. As an engineering student in college, Frank was exempt from being drafted, but he volunteered to join the Army anyway. He volunteered for one of the most dangerous units, the 101st Airborne Division, the legendary "Screaming Eagles."
That all changed on the night of Sunday, December 17th. Frank still remembers a sergeant interrupting everyone's sleep to announce that the German Army had broken through the front lines in Belgium. They were told to get up because they were heading out to join the fight in what would be known as the Battle of the Bulge. Over 600,000 American troops fought in the Battle of the Bulge, and it was the largest and bloodiest single battle fought by the US in World War II.

Dr. Tangherlini returned to the battlefield last December for the 75th anniversary of those defining days and shared seven lessons in leadership that sprang from that life-and-death experience:

1 - RECOGNITION is a Two-Way Gift – The 75th commemoration of the battle in Belgium was a big deal. He said he felt like one of the Beatles."
LEADERSHIP LESSON – We recognize the accomplishments of others to thank them and to share examples of what success looks like. But

another reason is we want to be a part of their success too. By recognizing others, we aren't just giving them a gift; we are getting a reward too.

2 - BE Flexible – Frank was an elite paratrooper trained to enter into a battle by jumping out of a plane. But he arrived at the Battle of the Bulge in a truck.
LEADERSHIP LESSON – Don't assume your job will go exactly like your job training told you it would. Be flexible enough to apply the core lessons you learned in any environment.

3 - ASK BEFORE ASSUMING – Frank's role was as an assistant machine gun operator, a member of a two-person team. He carried the tripod and ammunition while his partner carried the barrel. As they marched from the trucks to take a position on the periphery, his partner slipped and fell on the road. He was overloaded with too many grenades and equipment. Despite being trained to continue when others fell, Frank stopped, helped him up, and took some of his load. When he got to his position, the second lieutenant chewed Frank out for not following his training. Frank explained himself this way – "But sir, he had the other half of the machine gun." He figured that if he showed up with just the tripod, he would have been following the rules, but in a dumb way, since the barrel would have been left behind on the road.
LEADERSHIP LESSON - Frank summed up his decision to break from his training this way: "I did what I felt was the reasonable thing." My take - don't assume your folks are being unreasonable when they do something differently than the way you would do it.

4 - DEPUTIES MATTER
LEADERSHIP LESSON – Carefully select and groom a deputy. Everybody eventually has to hand over the reins at some point, expectedly or unexpectedly.

5 - COMMUNICATION IS CRITICAL
LEADERSHIP LESSON – The American troops camped out in foxholes learned about that "Nuts" reply quickly because McAuliffe had the surrender request and his response summarized in a statement that was distributed to his troops in the middle of the battle. That communication was made through paper copies made from something like a mimeograph machine – an old-fashioned copier machine that looks like a big desktop typewriter with a drum and a crank. At the 75th reunion, Frank got a replica of that paper distributed to soldiers during the battle. Whenever you think internal team communications isn't a critical need, remember that 101st Airborne troops somehow found room to haul along a simple paper copier machine when they deployed at the Battle of the Bulge.

6 – SECRECY IS SOMETIMES IMPORTANT TOO
LEADERSHIP LESSON – Communication is important, but not everybody needs to know everything.

7 – SAFETY FIRST –
LEADERSHIP LESSON – Job #1 in any workplace is safety, and leaders are responsible for ensuring the workspace is safe. It may not be as glamorous as the other parts of the job, but it is table stakes to do all the rest. "

In 1974, the commander of a military unit was the guest speaker at a graduation ceremony and was quoted as saying, "Leadership requires at least two parties: a leader and a follower." He went on to say that this seems evident; many attempts to lead meet with failure when the leader neglects the role of the follower. Attendees of this school numbered over 10,000, and their primary purpose is to prepare for future postings as new officers in the U.S. military forces.

In addition, thousands of civilian leaders are preparing to reach their goals as leaders of the organizations where they were recently hired to oversee a department. Let us also remember those who are opening their businesses. They, too, will, in their own unique way, attract customers to their stores. All these leaders must quickly earn trust and guide their teams with a clear purpose. Leadership starts with small, intentional actions that set the stage for success.

Many of us grow up believing in myths about leadership. It is to be expected that these myths will find their way into the literature and be promoted in leadership courses. For example, the animation shows children what it takes to be heroes and heroines. At one time, the Sunday Funnies were filled with examples, such as Wonder Woman, Superman, Buck Rogers, and Dick Tracy.

Now, most of us see these characters as truly mythical. But what about the sword in the stone, or calling King Arthur a king because he could pull the sword from the stone after many others failed? He was the natural leader, and only he could lead the kingdom. Or the myth that the biggest or strongest will lead. That childhood reasoning was what you used to pick who you wanted on your team.

Leadership doesn't happen naturally, nor does it develop overnight. It is a balanced combination of an individual's desire, training, and circumstances to lead, along with a group that needs guidance. Effective leadership is built through ongoing learning, self-awareness, and the ability to adapt to changing situations. It isn't about being the loudest or most dominant in the room but about listening, motivating, and making thoughtful decisions. True leaders empower others, foster inclusive environments, and lead by example rather than by command. They grow by learning from failure, staying humble in success, and remaining resilient through challenges.

A leader must have the vision to inspire others, the empathy to understand their needs, and the resilience to overcome challenges. By fostering a culture of trust and collaboration, leaders can motivate their team to reach shared goals. Leadership isn't just about directing others; it's about empowering them to reach their full potential and making a positive impact on the organization and beyond. It takes dedication, patience, and a genuine commitment to the growth and success of both the leader and their team. Great leaders also embrace continuous learning, adapting their approach as circumstances change. They listen actively, communicate openly, and lead by example, setting the standard for the behavior they expect. In doing so, they build not just teams, but communities of shared purpose and lasting success.

You can see that answering this question requires multiple perspectives. The fact is that leadership is a complex role that demands a mix of skills and abilities to guide and motivate others effectively. Here are some key skills and abilities that leaders have and how they demonstrate them:

Eliciting Cooperation

Leaders elicit cooperation by creating a shared vision and fostering a sense of purpose among their team members. They build trust and rapport, encouraging open communication and collaboration. By recognizing and valuing the contributions of others, leaders create an environment where everyone feels motivated to work towards common goals.

Effective Communication

Effective communication is crucial for leaders. They must be able to convey their ideas clearly and persuasively, both verbally and in writing. Leaders also listen actively, ensuring they understand the perspectives and concerns of their team members. This two-way communication helps build strong relationships and ensures that everyone is aligned.

Prioritizing Others

Leaders prioritize the needs of their team members by practicing empathy and showing genuine concern for their well-being. They empower others by providing the necessary resources and support, and by recognizing and celebrating their achievements. This approach not only boosts morale but also fosters a culture of trust and collaboration.

Most of us agree that these three character traits are highly desirable in a leader. However, this leads us to think about the natural leader versus the gifted leader. What does someone need? Can it be developed?

Enhancing leadership skills is crucial for personal and professional growth. Most authorities agree that three fundamental pillars are necessary for this quest to be accomplished. The new leader must be trained. What will be the goal of this leader, and finally, who will follow this leader? All are equally important. There are numerous development strategies, subjects, subcomponents, and methodologies for building these skills.

Five Critical Strategies That Build Leaders

Self-awareness and Emotional Intelligence

Self-awareness, or Emotional Intelligence as defined by Daniel Goleman in his popular book, Emotional Intelligence 2.0, is the ability to recognize and understand one's own emotions, thoughts, and behaviors. It involves being conscious of your strengths, weaknesses, values, and motivations. Self-aware leaders are better equipped to make informed decisions, manage stress effectively, and communicate more clearly. Key aspects of self-awareness include emotional awareness, which involves recognizing your own emotions and their impact on your thoughts and actions; accurate self-assessment, which helps you set realistic goals and seek appropriate development opportunities; and self-confidence, which enables you to take on challenges and lead with conviction.

Emotional intelligence (EI) is the ability to perceive, understand, manage, and regulate emotions in oneself and others. It is vital for building and maintaining healthy relationships, resolving conflicts, and creating a positive work environment. In today's complex and fast-paced world, EI is a crucial leadership skill that builds trust and encourages effective collaboration. Key elements of EI include self-regulation, which involves managing and controlling one's emotions, particularly in stressful situations; motivation, which drives leaders to pursue goals for internal reasons rather than external rewards; empathy, which allows leaders to understand and share the feelings of others; and social skills, which enable effective interactions, strengthen relationships, and help manage social networks.

Communication Skills

Practical communication skills are vital for effective interaction and teamwork. Key components include active listening, which means fully concentrating, understanding, responding to, and remembering what is being said; non-verbal communication, which involves understanding and using body language, facial expressions, and gestures; public speaking, which is about effectively conveying ideas and information to an audience; and conflict resolution, which centers on managing and resolving conflicts constructively.

To develop these skills, various methods can be used. Attending workshops on communication skills, such as active listening and public speaking, can be very helpful. Joining groups like Toastmasters offers chances to practice and enhance public speaking skills. Participating in simulation exercises helps practice conflict resolution and non-verbal communication. Additionally, doing peer reviews allows for receiving helpful feedback on communication skills.

Strategic Thinking and Decision Making

Strategic thinking and decision-making are essential skills for effective leadership. Problem-solving involves quickly identifying and addressing issues, while critical thinking requires analyzing and evaluating information to make well-informed decisions. Visioning means creating a clear and inspiring picture of the future, while risk management involves assessing and reducing risks related to decisions. These components together enhance a leader's ability to handle complex situations and promote organizational success.

To develop these skills, various methods can be used. Analyzing case studies helps understand different approaches to strategic thinking and decision-making. Participating in scenario planning exercises allows leaders to anticipate and prepare for potential future challenges. Learning and applying decision-making models can improve the quality of decisions. Seeking mentorship from experienced leaders provides valuable insights into strategic thinking and decision-making, enhancing a leader's ability to make sound decisions and lead effectively.

Team Building and Collaboration

Team building and collaboration are vital for developing a unified and efficient work environment. Building trust involves creating confidence within the team, which is essential for successful collaboration. Delegation means assigning tasks and responsibilities properly so team members can deliver their best work. Motivation aims to inspire and encourage team members to excel, while conflict management focuses on addressing and resolving disagreements to keep harmony and productivity.

To develop these skills, various methodologies can be employed. Organizing team retreats helps to build trust and strengthen relationships among team members. Engaging in group projects provides opportunities to practice delegation and collaboration. Regular team check-ins can identify challenges early and encourage shared accountability. Participating in motivational workshops can inspire and energize the team, while attending conflict resolution training sessions equips team members with the skills to manage and resolve conflicts constructively. Regular feedback sessions foster open communication and continuous improvement, which are vital for team growth.

Continuous Learning and Adaptability

Continuous learning and adaptability are crucial for effective leadership. Lifelong learning involves a commitment to ongoing development and staying updated with the latest trends and knowledge. Adaptability requires flexibility and openness to change, while innovation encourages creativity within the team. Leaders who embrace change set a positive example that motivates their teams to follow suit. Establishing a continuous feedback loop is crucial for enhancing performance and cultivating a culture of growth.

To develop these skills, various methods can be used. Enrolling in online courses helps leaders stay updated with the latest information and techniques. Regularly reading books, articles, and journals related to leadership and management offers valuable insights. Attending workshops and seminars provides opportunities to acquire new skills, and engaging in peer learning sessions enables the sharing of knowledge and experiences. Consistently reflecting on feedback and experiences enables leaders to refine their approach and grow stronger over time.

This document highlights important leadership qualities and strategies, focusing on transparency, effective delegation, and continuous learning. Transparent leaders build trust through openness and honesty; for example, a leader might share the company's financial status and plans with the team to foster trust and alignment. Effective delegation makes sure tasks are completed efficiently; for instance, a project manager might assign specific roles based on team members' strengths, ensuring the most capable person handles each task. Continuous learning helps leaders stay adaptable and informed; a leader might regularly attend industry conferences or enroll in online courses to stay updated with the latest trends and knowledge, helping navigate the complexities of a rapidly changing business environment. Leaders should consistently model these behaviors to shape team culture. Only through continuous practice and modeling can these qualities become ingrained, creating a culture of excellence and shared responsibility.

Chapter 2
The Leadership Mysteries Enigma

"True wisdom comes to each of us when we realize how little we understand about life, ourselves, and the world around us," --- Socrates.

One of the topics that is at the center of discussion in academic and intellectual circles is leadership. For some time, this subject has been explored in ways never seen before. Sadly, many people around us claim to be leaders or are called such by those in their immediate circles. But do they truly have what it takes to lead? Maybe yes, maybe no. Remember, authentic leadership often requires us to adapt and grow in response to the challenges we face.

Before you continue, ask yourself what others would say your style is. How would you describe your leadership style? Does it stay the same regardless of the situation?

Thirteen Well-known leaders and their styles:

CHARISMA

CHARISMA EXAMPLES
Oprah Winfrey used a charismatic style of leadership to build a global media empire.
Others: **Dolly Parton, John F. Kennedy**

If you're looking for an example of a charismatic leader, here is a one-word hint: Oprah. She has won over her following so thoroughly that she is known worldwide by a single name. Charismatic leaders connect on a personal level and convey an extraordinary sensitivity to people's needs.

PARTICIPATIVE

PARTICIPATIVE EXAMPLES
Carlos Ghosn is CEO of Renault and Nissan. One company is based in France, the other in Japan.

Other: **Eleanor Roosevelt**

How would you like to lead an organization where employees are fully engaged and regularly bring new ideas to the table, then eagerly await your approval to run with them? This is a style of leadership in which the leader involves subordinates in goal setting, problem-solving, team building, and other activities, but **retains the final decision-making authority.**

AUTHORITARIAN

AUTHORITARIAN EXAMPLES
Margaret Thatcher, the British Prime Minister known as the "Iron Lady," relied on this style.

Others: **Napoleon, Bill Gates, co-founder of Microsoft,**

Ever wonder what would happen if you tried to lead by yelling and screaming and stomping? How about threats? It **worked for Napoleon**. It's working right now for Kim Jong-un in North Korea. It appears to work for Donald Trump, at least on television. In a nutshell, that's the authoritarian leadership style, and while it has its shortcomings, it also **has a long history of success, albeit often short-lived.**

COACHING

COACHING EXAMPLES
Barbara Walters mentored Oprah Winfrey. "If there had not been you, there never would have been me," says Oprah.

Other: **Andrew Carnegie** aided U.S. Steel's Charles Schwab

Coaching is a leadership style that develops people by **offering hands-on advice for problem-solving**. If this style were summed up in a phrase, it would be "Try this." The coaching style is most effective when the leader aims to help staff develop lasting personal and professional strengths that enhance their overall success.

AFFILIATIVE

AFFILIATIVE EXAMPLES
Joe Torre, former NY Yankees manager, won 4 World Series by using this style to manage the egos of talented players.
Other: **Maharishi Mahesh Yogi,** guru to The Beatles

An affiliative leader fosters harmony among their followers, with a strong focus on resolving **interpersonal conflicts.** This type of leader will also build teams that ensure their followers feel connected. This leader is **a master at establishing positive relationships.**

TRANSFORMATIONAL

TRANSFORMATIONAL EXAMPLES
Dalai Lama doesn't seek power over others, but seeks to inspire others to join the cause to restore Tibet's freedom.
Others: **Teddy Roosevelt, John D. Rockefeller**

Good leadership consists of showing average people
how to do the work of superior people.
— *John D. Rockefeller*

Transformational leadership boosts morale, motivation, and performance by **creating a unified sense of identity and purpose for a project and encouraging people to embrace and participate in** it. Think e pluribus unum – "from many, one."

BUREAUCRATIC

BUREAUCRATIC EXAMPLES
Gunnery Sergeant Hartman, played by R. Lee Ermey in "Full Metal Jacket", was the ultimate bureaucratic leader.

Others: **No one wants to admit to being a bureaucrat**

Bureaucratic leadership is most commonly on display in large, classically corporate organizations. Think U.S. Army, actor R. Lee Ermey in Full Metal Jacket. The bureaucratic style is born out of a **mandatory obedience to authority that is both ingrained and enforced over time**. "Followers" do as they are told because it is both easier and safer to follow the chain of command.

EMERGENT

EMERGENT EXAMPLES
Sergey Brin, co-founder of Google, wasn't looking to build a company. But he emerged as a leader as Google grew.

Other: **Mark Zuckerberg,** co-founder of Facebook

When someone begins taking on tasks voluntarily, helping others do their jobs better, and encouraging consensus among co-workers, this person is an emergent leader. This type of leadership is distinguished by the leader **stepping up before being formally given a leadership title.** Emergent leaders make it clear by their actions that they are ready for the next promotion.

LAISSEZ-FAIRE

LAISSEZ-FAIRE EXAMPLES
Warren Buffett takes a hands-off approach and his managers are motivated by the great latitude he gives them.

Others: **Richard Branson (Virgin Group), Herbert Hoover**

Laissez-faire leaders steer clear of sweeping policies. Instead, groups or individuals are left to make responsible decisions and solve problems.

Successful laissez-faire leadership is built on trust and **works best when the leader oversees a highly trained and reliable group of people.**

SITUATIONAL

SITUATIONAL EXAMPLES
Abraham Lincoln used more than one style, but slavery and the Civil War dictated he be a situational leader.
Others: Winston Churchill, Gen. George Patton

Situation leadership is what you do when you practice every style of leadership on this page in situations that require. Situational leaders do not stick to a single style but adjust their leadership approach as needed. They not only modify themselves and their personal styles, but they may also need to change goals, responsibilities, and tasks based on the group's experience and performance.

PACESETTER

PACESETTER EXAMPLES
Elon Musk, co-founder of PayPal and CEO of startups SpaceX and Tesla, is always pushing to grow.
Others: George Washington, Jack Welch of GE

Pacesetters are driven to accomplish tasks more efficiently and effectively. On the surface, there is a lot to admire about that quality. But when you look beneath, there can be a lot of baggage that comes with being a Pacesetter.

These people set high standards for themselves and others. What's more, they'd never ask others to do something they wouldn't do. Sounds great, for a while.

SERVANT LEADERSHIP

SERVANT EXAMPLES
Herb Kelleher, founder of SouthWest Airlines, who said, "The business of business is people."

Others: **Sister Teresa, Albert Schweitzer**

A servant leader is someone, regardless of level, who **leads simply by meeting the needs of the team**. The term sometimes describes a person without formal recognition as a leader. These individuals often set a good example. They possess a high level of integrity and lead with generosity. Their approach can foster a positive corporate culture and boost morale among team members.

COERCIVE LEADERSHIP

COERCIVE EXAMPLES
Sheldon Cooper, played by actor Jim Parsons in "The Big Bang Theory." With him, the only right way is Sheldon's way.

Other: **Joseph Stalin,** former leader of the Soviet Union

This person rules by fear. "My way or the highway!" They **take charge and invite no contrary opinions.** Many **organizations in serious trouble have gone to this style as a last resort.** A significant downside is that once the crisis resolves itself and the coercive style continues unchecked, it will create other problems of its own.

First, we need to differentiate between leadership and effective leadership. Contrary to popular belief, management is not just about overseeing tasks, supervising teams, and ensuring that things get done. While these elements are important to leadership, much more lies beneath the surface. A key trait of an effective leader is the ability to empower the team to reach their full potential as employees and collaborators. Effective leaders focus on developing people rather than simply managing processes. They understand that long-term success comes from building trust, encouraging creativity, and offering growth opportunities. When individuals feel appreciated and challenged, they give their best effort, fostering both personal and organizational growth.

Through his vision, he fosters an environment where everyone is a winner, whether they are the boss or an employee. It is very rare for someone to develop and succeed without mentoring, coaching, or guidance. In personal life, it's possible, but within an organizational hierarchy, you must both lead and follow, making leadership essential. You may be highly talented and charismatic as a leader, but what truly matters is how you interact with your teammates and whether you help them grow. A leader should always be prepared to mentor, train, and inspire their team in ways that enable them to advance and become leaders themselves. Some key needs for individuals are clarity, space, and information. Most importantly, it is the leader's responsibility to provide these elements. Through this process, not only does the team learn and grow, but the leader also learns and evolves alongside them.

In the following paragraphs, we will first identify some of the most common traits of an ineffective leader: Poor Communication Skills, Lack Of Conviction, Unwillingness To Change, Poor Relationship Building, Poor Task Management, No Significant Results, And Poor Employee Development.

Ineffective Leaders

Poor Communication Skills

If you aspire to become a leader, it is essential to

understand that effective communication is key. If you cannot or will not communicate clearly and appropriately with your team at the right time, all your efforts will be futile. A common trait of a leader lacking communication skills is trying to speak as much as possible, which can overwhelm subordinates. Many fail to realize that communication is a two-way process. To be a good communicator, you must also be a good listener. Unfortunately, some people believe they don't need to listen to their team members, thinking they already have enough knowledge. By not listening, they miss important points that could be crucial for discussions and future solutions. When that happens, the doors to new ideas, Opportunities and possibilities are cut off, which can severely slow progress. Also, these individuals display unapproachable body language, discouraging others from sharing their opinions and ideas. As a result, those ideas often face their most painful ending.

Lastly, when asked to address a group from a stage, they frequently lack confidence, sometimes trembling, and tend to read from a script instead of sharing their views confidently.

Lack of

Some people often confuse leadership weakness with a lack of strength, which is understandable, but it's not the only factor. One reason a leader may appear weak is the absence of conviction, confidence, and resolve. When in a leadership position, the individuals you are responsible for need vision and empowerment. At times, they even require the truth, which can be beneficial for their growth. Sharing the truth represents transparency. When a leader is confident and adheres to their convictions, a strong team is formed, with all members collaborating and supporting one another in times of need. Conversely, if the leader lacks confidence and resolve, the team may frequently succumb to nervousness, uncertainty, dishonesty, and insecurity. True leadership begins with self-assurance. When a leader believes in their purpose, it sets the tone for the entire team's mindset and behavior.

Unwillingness to Change

On the other hand, an ineffective leader is either unable or unwilling to change. When it is time to adapt, they shy away or panic, causing things to spiral downward, ultimately resulting in chaos. With poor leadership, even the smallest adjustments become painstaking. Let's face it: the only constant in our lives is change. We will discuss the change in greater detail in Chapter 8. It is the only way forward, and the sooner you understand this, the better off you'll be. Adapting to change can be tricky and requires making tough decisions. However, as an effective leader, you know how to navigate such situations. A true leader welcomes change with open arms, and so does their team. A professional doesn't shy away from temporary challenges; instead, they seek timely solutions to problems rather than giving up and succumbing to pressure. As a result, they continue to move forward and achieve specific benchmarks that others can only dream of. When a leader is open to change, they foster a proactive environment. People embrace change because it offers countless learning opportunities.

Poor Relationship Building

An incompetent leader resorts to criticism rather than encouragement, resulting in more foes than friends. Furthermore, when you are not skilled at building relationships, you create an unfavorable organizational culture that does not benefit you or your team members. This toxic environment stifles creativity, lowers morale, and drives talented individuals away.

Whether it's a personal or professional relationship, it

requires a lot of work. Building and maintaining such relationships takes time, and they don't develop overnight. When these relationships are strengthened, respect and trust are born. However, cultivating a healthy relationship requires a lot of patience. That is when we truly distinguish between a good leader and a bad one. A good leader possesses the patience needed to maintain relationships over extended periods, while a bad one tends to become frustrated and infuriated over trivial matters, thus missing the chance to establish a beneficial relationship with followers in the future. Strong leaders also invest time in understanding their team's individual needs and aspirations, fostering loyalty and a shared sense of purpose.

There are frequently real-world opportunities to reinforce the learning here. A notable real-world example was the Ford Motor Company's decision to reallocate its resources to produce much-needed medical equipment, such as ventilators, to support hospitalized COVID-19 patients. Those team members knew they made a difference in people's lives, and by the same notion, they made a difference in their own lives.

Poor Task Management

Another flaw of a poor task manager is assigning tasks that exceed the capabilities and skill sets of their team members. In contrast, a good leader recognizes the strengths and weaknesses of their team and assigns tasks accordingly. Task management is a crucial aspect of leadership. Effective task managers not only establish priorities but also set boundaries. They also eliminate distractions and obstacles that hinder productivity, especially when working under tight deadlines.

Additionally, a leader who struggles with task management often assigns too many people to a single task, which is usually unhelpful and can, in many cases, become extremely problematic. A leader should excel at task management as well as the distribution and delegation of work. The leader must be acutely aware of which task to assign and to whom. This careful balance allows the team to remain productive and helps prevent burnout.

No Significant Results

The purpose of leadership is to get things done. Additionally, failing to build relationships, a lack of funding, insufficient resources, and unrealistic expectations can lead to poor results. An ineffective leader often lacks essential technical knowledge. These leaders also struggle with decision-making and may avoid making decisions altogether, resorting to numerous unrealistic excuses instead.

At the heart of it all lies a lack of confidence and fear, which paralyzes their ability to make decisions, forcing the team to adhere to whatever they choose. Ultimately, they are left empty-handed, with nothing significant to show for their efforts. The absence of results severely impacts the organization, jeopardizing their jobs in the long run. Results are the bottom line for a leader, and achieving those outcomes is not guaranteed for anyone in that role. Those who accomplish their mission and deliver results embody at least two fundamental aspects of leadership: 1) understanding that holding the position only makes you a boss at best. A boss doesn't do all the work, which makes the second aspect critical. Fostering connections and relationships with the team. Teamwork is essential for achieving success and accomplishing missions.

Poor Employee Development

Conversely, an inadequate and incompetent leader rarely considers anything of substance, especially employee development. This individual is least concerned about whether the team is growing and progressing. Often, they don't even care about their vital role in the organization's advancement.

A visionary leader looks at the bigger picture. Their clear desire is for the company to grow, and for team members to grow alongside it. Therefore, techniques to train and develop the workforce so they can handle competition effectively and benefit the company in the long run are top of mind for the leader. Additionally, an effective leader invests in activities, seminars, and workshops focused on employee training and development.

The Effective Leaders Know Themselves

<u>Techniques and Tools for Self-Discovery.</u> To paraphrase Michael Jackson, if you want change, first look at the person in the mirror. So far, we have looked at some traits of an ineffective leader. However, before you can become a capable leader and learn to manage things effectively and efficiently, you need to focus on yourself as an individual. In doing so, you should build on your strengths while working to improve your weaknesses to prevent them from becoming obstacles (we will discuss more about identifying your strengths later). For quite some time now, humans have been trying to understand how they arrived here, both individually and as a society. Before addressing a group or the community as a whole, it's essential to have a conversation with the individual. We also need to understand the factors that influence people on a personal level. Some of these factors include:

- Norms of the family
- Our peers
- The groups we're associated with
- Supervisors
- The organizations

- A person's skillset

Before choosing a career or applying for a job, you need to understand your interests, strengths, weaknesses, and areas that need improvement. Over time, experts have developed some simple techniques people can use to better understand themselves before entering the workforce and interacting with others. How we view ourselves is especially important because it influences how we perceive and engage with other people.

On the flip side, if you think poorly of yourself, you'll also think poorly of others. If you respect yourself, your choices, and your opinions, you'll extend similar respect to those you meet, whether they are friends, family members, people on campus, or colleagues. Over time, experts have developed several techniques that help individuals gain a clear and vivid picture of their actual personality type.

Other than that, some excellent pieces of literature cover how an individual can focus on using their strengths while working on areas for improvement. In providing these snapshots of some of my favorite personal instruments, I have two cautions for you when using survey or assessment instruments. Always work with a professional career advisor when selecting and using these instruments.

Let's analyze it step by step.

Personal Assessment Instruments
MBTI

MBTI stands for Myers-Briggs Type Indicator. Long ago, Isabel Myers and her mother, Katherine Briggs, began working on Carl Jung's theory of personality types. It was first published in 1944 as the Briggs Myers Type Indicator and was later renamed the Myers-Briggs Type Indicator in

1956. The instruments themselves were published in 1962. Today, it is one of the most popular personality assessment tools worldwide. It helps individuals understand their personality type, strengths, weaknesses, and preferences.

Now, let's examine the four different scales of measurement used by the test. Before diving into the four scales, it's essential to understand that no personality type is better or worse than another. Additionally, these scales combine to form 16 unique personality types. Therefore, your specific combination of these four scales determines your type, such as ESTJ, INFP, or ENFJ.

- Extraversion (E) - Introversion (I): The concept of extraversion and introversion was first introduced by Carl Jung in his personality types theory. It specifically focuses on how a person interacts with those around them. Extraverts generally enjoy social situations and are good at meeting new people. In contrast, introverts tend to avoid social issues and feel more comfortable being alone. Neither type is better than the other, and both have their strengths.

- Sensing (S) vs. Intuition (N): This scale focuses on how people gather information from the world around them. People who favor sensing tend to pay close attention to their immediate realities and trust what they can learn from their five senses. In contrast, intuitive people look for patterns and impressions. They are more interested in possibilities and abstract ideas.

- Thinking (T)-Feeling (F): The previous scale focuses on gathering information, while this one centers on decision-making after collecting that information. Thinkers tend to prioritize facts and objective data. They do not trust anything until it can be proven numerically. Conversely, people usually base their decisions on emotions and relationships.

- Perceiving (P)-Judging (J): The last scale on our list highlights how a person interacts with the world around them. People who prefer judging tend to make firm decisions and follow structured plans. In contrast, those who lean toward perceiving are generally more open, flexible, and adaptable when engaging with the outside world.

The MBTI personality types are listed below

ISTJ - The Inspector
ISTP - The Crafter
ISFJ – The Protector
ISFP - The Artist
INFJ - The Advocate
INFP - The Mediator
INTJ - The Architect
INTP - The Thinker

ESTP - The Persuader
ESTJ - The Director
ESFP - The Performer
ESFJ - The Caregiver
ENFP - The Champion
ENFJ - The Giver
ENTP - The Debater
ENTJ - The Commander

Strong Interest Inventory Test

According to this test (initially published in 1927), people find ways to connect their interests, likes, and preferences with their academics, work, and leisure activities. It helps them understand what they would like to do at work and during their free time. This test is further divided into categories, which are as follows.

General Occupations Themes: This category offers an economic framework for a strong inventory interest profile.

It also explains a person's overall attitude toward a particular field of work.

Basic Interest Scales: This is an additional means of explaining both low and high scores on the General Occupational Theme Scales. Doing so measures a person's inbuilt penchant for a particular activity or even a specific subject.

Occupational Scales: These scales lay the foundation of the Strong Interest Inventory test. These scales tend to connect some specific interests with particular occupations.

Personal Style Scales: This category generally measures comfort with various broad styles of living and working. It also focuses on how a person prefers to be taught and how they like to complete work-related tasks. Additionally, it considers whether a person needs to be alone or surrounded by others to be successful at a work-related job.

Let's move forward and take a look at the jobs that are suitable for specific people.

Jobs of *Realistic-Favoring people* are as follows:
- Carpenter
- Auto Mechanic
- Forester
- Engineer
- Technician
- Law Enforcement Officer

Here are some of the hobbies for such individuals:
- Hunting
- Camping
- Auto Repairing
- Motorcycles
- Mountain Climbing
- Skydiving
- Reading

Then some people are *Investigative Favoring*. The best jobs for them are as follows:
- Computer Engineer
- Psychologist
- Geologist
- Inspector/Detective
- Vet
- Professor
- Physician

The best hobbies for such people are as follows:
- Reading
- Sailing
- Astronomy
- Scuba Diving
- Playing Chess

Then, some people are more *artistic in nature*. The perfect jobs for them are as follows:
- Playing music
- Architecture
- Film-making
- Direction/Production
- Sculpturing
- Being a Painter
- Graphic Design
- Photography

Interestingly, their hobbies sometimes overlap with their work, which is okay and perfectly alright:
- Photography
- Playing the piano, guitar, or any other instrument
- Reading
- Going to concerts and art exhibitions
- Frequenting the theater
- Composing their own poetry or prose

Some people have a *social-favoring nature.* The best jobs for them are as follows:
- Schoolteacher
- Social Activist
- Social Worker
- Speech Therapist
- Social Science Teacher
- Nurse
- Doctor

Gallup's StrengthsFinder 2.0

One of the latest surveys on personality assessment is Gallup's StrengthsFinder 2.0 (first published in 2007). It is one of the most straightforward tools that help you understand the strengths of the people currently working on your team. Once you identify the strengths and aptitudes of your team members, you can leverage and maximize them. At the same time, you can boost your team members' productivity and morale, leading to excellent results. Some of the benefits of using StrengthsFinder 2.0 are as follows.

- One of the top benefits of this new technique is that it allows you to assign people to roles where they fit best within your organization. You also find it easier to identify the roles they can fulfill. As a result, employee performance becomes more innovative and creative; at the same time, employers will be more satisfied with their work. Additionally, it boosts employee engagement, which is crucial given the changing landscape of the professional world. This tool is especially useful during the hiring process. It helps you evaluate from the start whether candidates can grow and develop within the positions they are being considered for. Moreover, there's a small chance that new hires won't perform well in their initial roles. That's where this tool comes into play; it helps you determine the best placement for them.

• Furthermore, it lays the foundation for effective coaching within the organization. It allows you to focus on people's strengths and capitalize on them, rather than being too obsessed and occupied with their weaknesses. When it comes to giving feedback, you can relate their success to their strengths while helping them out in areas where they aren't inherently strong.

Your employees' strengths can be used as a yardstick to measure high and low performance and identify what can be done to troubleshoot the underlying problems. To make the person learn more and grow as an individual within the organization, more challenging tasks should be assigned, and they should be in perfect accordance with the strengths that you have just identified.

• Moreover, StrengthsFinder 2.0 aids in the individualization of management. When managing large teams, you can't truly rely on a one-size-fits-all approach. Each employee may react differently to a new management style. What works well for one person may not be as effective for the rest of the team. Conversely, when a manager is aware of the team's individual strengths and weaknesses, finding an effective leadership style that suits all team members becomes much easier.

• Another benefit of this survey is that it facilitates collaboration. When working on diverse projects, it is important to have team members who bring something new and different to the table.

• As a result, you can create teams that work well together. Moreover, it helps to resolve conflicts and understand why some people behave a certain way in specific situations.

• Lastly, this tool helps improve self-awareness. On an individual level, it is highly beneficial.

For a person to understand their strengths and weaknesses. As a result, the person can understand the critical developmental needs.

The Ideal Team Player and His Virtues

Jeff Shanely was the co-founder of a Silicon Valley startup. At some point, while looking to change his career, an opportunity arose to take over the family business. It was a construction company with many options, but the biggest challenge was creating a culture of teamwork within the company.

The case discussed in the previous paragraph is the premise that Patrick Lencioni's book (2016) The Ideal Team Player: How to Recognize and Cultivate the Three Essential Virtues focuses on. In this book, the three virtues of an ideal team player are explained. These virtues are Humility, Hunger, and Smarts. It should be noted that these traits are not innate, and team players are not born with them. Instead, these traits can be developed through their skills, preferences, interests, and life experiences. When a team member is missing any one of these virtues, it can make things particularly challenging.

Humility

The most important virtue on our list is Humility. According to this book, an ideal team player doesn't have a grand and arrogant ego that defines who they are and what they do. They aren't conceited and don't seek recognition for their efforts. Additionally, they're able to appreciate others and acknowledge their contributions. To them, success isn't something to be celebrated alone. Instead, it is something earned through the collective effort of the whole team. A person who lacks Humility is immediately disqualified from being an ideal team player.

Hunger

Another virtue of ideal team players is their hunger. Here, hunger doesn't refer to the physiological need for food; instead, it relates to the drive that a person has for new opportunities and possibilities. Such individuals have a penchant for learning and willingly take on more responsibility. Because they are self-motivated and diligent, they do not require extra pushing to perform well. Without hunger, a person cannot succeed.

Smarts

In this book, being smart has little to do with a person's intellectual ability. Conversely, a smart team player has good common sense about the people around them. They pay close attention to what's happening within the team and look for ways to handle situations effectively. Additionally, they communicate well and tend to listen more than they speak. They also ask questions, which helps them learn about others and their personalities. They aim to avoid problems and conflicts to keep things as peaceful as possible. Your success is often connected to an individual's and an organization's ability to lead and manage change.

Effective Communication

If you want to emerge as a market leader within your niche and beat your competition, you aren't alone. If that's the case, you need to foster a culture within your organization where all team members connect on a deeper level. However, this is easier said than done. If you ensure effective communication within your organization, it shouldn't be too difficult. If you are in charge, you can train your team to be effective communicators. At the same time, you need to lead by example and engage in effective communication with your team members and subordinates.

Here are some of the essential components of an effective communication that you can't afford to skimp.

- First on our list is effective listening. Communication is a two-way process. You can't expect to talk without taking the time to listen to the other person's viewpoint. You may be a master of your craft, but the possibility of improvement cannot be overlooked. When you listen to the other person attentively, you open yourself up to a whole new world of options and opportunities that can benefit your organization. Moreover, it makes your employees feel cared for and valued.

- As important as speaking and listening are, so is non-verbal communication. Some claim that 80% of communication is non-verbal. One of the critical components of non-verbal communication is body language. When you communicate, your body should face the other person. Good eye contact and a slight smile can help you go the distance. Additionally, when you listen, make sure to nod. Nodding enables you to make the other person realize that they are conveying their message effectively.

- When you communicate, make sure you keep the message straightforward, direct, and as concise as possible. Do not mask your words with unnecessary talk.

- Also, when you communicate, you should make the other person feel respected. Even if you are their senior officer and have more experience in the field, it is important to make them feel valued. Pay close attention to what they have to say, even if you are the one making the final decision.

- Open-mindedness is key to effective communication. The person you are talking to might have different viewpoints on most matters. Still, you should learn to celebrate those differences rather than allowing them to become an obstruction to your communication. Learn to accept and embrace the differences, thus creating a more progressive workplace.
- Last on our list is empathy. Empathy closely relates to respect and open-mindedness. Simple phrases like "I get your point" or "I completely understand what you have been through" can make a difference. They help the other person see that their opinions are valued and that you fully understand their perspective while also appreciating their background.

Empathy in Communication

As discussed earlier, empathy plays a crucial role in effective communication. Some ways to demonstrate more empathy during a conversation include these, and some may even overlap with the elements mentioned above.

- Listen more and talk less. Give the other person a chance to speak rather than bombard them with your opinions.
- Try to form a connection with the other person.
- Allow the other person to present their opinions first.
- Let them know that you have understood their take on the issue before you move on.
- Remember, empathy has an emotional component to it. Learn to feel where the other person is coming from.

Continuing Options:

The following list of opportunities for employees should be included in an ongoing development program.

1. To Be A Mentor To An Employee.
2. Three-Letter Employee Fill-In For You And Staff Meetings.
3. Five Allow Employees To Pursue And Develop Any Idea They Have.
4. Senior Employee To Attend A Seminar On A New Topic.
5. Bringing Employees Along When You Call on Customers.

Allow An Employee To Shadow You During Your Workday.

Chapter 3
Developing Innovative and Inclusive Leadership Competencies

"Leadership is not about being in charge.
It's about taking care of those in your charge."
--- Simon Sinek

Developing inclusive leadership skills is essential for driving successful I & I initiatives. It involves leaders reflecting on their biases, gaining a thorough understanding of inclusion, and dedicating themselves to creating an inclusive culture within their organizations.

Reinforcing strategies

In addition to looking in the mirror, several other strategies can strengthen the case for inclusive leadership.

Education and Awareness: Leaders should participate in educational opportunities to deepen their understanding of I & I principles and practices. The initial focus should be on personal and professional courses, workshops, and seminars. The core areas should expand individual knowledge about unconscious bias, cultural competence, inclusive leadership, and allyship. For example, a leader might attend a workshop on unconscious bias to learn about how biases affect decision-making and strategies to reduce them. They could then apply these strategies in their daily interactions and decisions. Ongoing learning not only improves leadership effectiveness but also demonstrates a true commitment to creating an inclusive and fair environment.

Self-Reflection and Feedback: Encourage leaders to engage in self-reflection and seek feedback from a variety of perspectives. This process helps leaders recognize their biases, blind spots, and areas for development. They can use 360-degree feedback assessments to gain insights into their leadership behaviors and how these influence inclusivity. For example, a leader might utilize a 360-degree feedback tool to collect input from colleagues, subordinates, and peers about their leadership style and potential improvements. This feedback can then be used to create a personalized plan to enhance their inclusive leadership skills.

Mentoring and Coaching: Offer leaders mentoring and coaching support to help them develop inclusive leadership. Experienced mentors and coaches can assist leaders in overcoming challenges, acquiring new skills, and creating action plans to incorporate inclusive practices into their leadership approach. For example, a leader might work with a mentor experienced in diversity and inclusion. The mentor can guide them on handling difficult conversations about race and gender, suggest strategies for fostering an inclusive team culture, and assist in setting development goals.

Employee Resource Groups (ERGs): Involve leaders in collaboration with ERGs. By participating in ERG events and initiatives, leaders can gain firsthand insights into the experiences and perspectives of diverse employees. This involvement promotes empathy, understanding, and a stronger commitment to inclusion. For example, a leader might attend an ERG meeting for LGBTQ+ employees, where they listen to the challenges faced by these employees and learn about initiatives to support them. This experience helps the leader better understand the needs of LGBTQ+ employees and advocate for policies that promote their inclusion.

Cross-Cultural Experiences: Encourage leaders to pursue cross-cultural opportunities, such as international assignments, job rotations, or exposure to diverse communities. These experiences expand their perspectives and improve their ability to lead inclusively in a multicultural setting. For example, a leader might take part in a job rotation program that involves working in a different country for six months. During this period, they can learn about the local culture, build relationships with colleagues from different backgrounds, and develop a greater appreciation for cultural differences.

Unconscious Bias Training: Assisting leaders in identifying and reducing unconscious biases that can influence decision-making and hinder inclusivity. For example, a leader might attend a training session that incorporates interactive exercises to reveal common biases and their consequences. They can then implement the skills gained to limit bias in their hiring and promotion choices.

Cultural Competence Training: Building an understanding of diverse cultural norms, values, and practices to promote inclusive communication and teamwork. For instance, a leader might participate in a cultural competence training where they learn about the communication styles and work preferences of various cultural groups. This knowledge can help them adjust their communication and leadership style to better support team members from different backgrounds.

Inclusive Leadership Training: Prepares leaders with the knowledge and skills to manage diverse teams, build inclusive workplaces, and harness diversity for innovation and success. For example, a leader might take part in a training program that emphasizes inclusive leadership practices, such as creating a safe space for team members to share ideas, recognizing and valuing different perspectives, and fostering a culture of collaboration and respect.

Ongoing Learning and Growth: Promoting recurring training to emphasize the importance of continuous learning and development. This includes offering regular refresher courses, providing access to resources such as articles, podcasts, and videos on I & I-related topics, and supporting peer learning and sharing of best practices among leaders. For example, a leader might subscribe to a monthly newsletter that shares the latest research and best practices in diversity and inclusion. They can also participate in quarterly webinars to stay informed about emerging trends and strategies.

Implementing these strategies

By implementing these strategies and providing comprehensive training opportunities, organizations can empower leaders to develop inclusive leadership competencies, ensuring that I & I initiatives are effectively supported and advanced throughout the organization.

1. Staying Current: Ongoing training helps managers stay updated with the latest industry trends, best practices, and emerging technologies. This knowledge allows them to make well-informed decisions and lead their teams effectively in a rapidly changing business environment.

2. Enhancing Leadership Skills: Training offers opportunities for managers to improve their leadership abilities, such as communication, conflict resolution, decision-making, and strategic thinking. These technical and strategic skills are crucial for effectively leading teams and driving organizational success.

3. Adapting to Change: Training provides managers with the skills to handle change and uncertainty. It helps them lead their teams through organizational shifts, embrace new technologies, and react effectively to market changes.

4. Fostering Employee Engagement: Leaders who invest in continuous training show their dedication to employee growth and development. This promotes a culture of learning and involvement, boosting employee satisfaction and retention.

5. Building Emotional Intelligence: Training in areas like empathy, active listening, and relationship management helps managers develop emotional intelligence. This skill is essential for effective leadership, as it improves communication, teamwork, and employee motivation.

6. Managing Diversity and Inclusion: Ongoing training helps managers develop the knowledge and skills to lead diverse

and inclusive teams. It improves their cultural competence, reduces unconscious bias, and enables them to create inclusive work environments where everyone feels valued and heard.

7. Nurturing Innovation: Training encourages managers to think creatively and fosters an environment that supports innovation. It equips them with techniques for generating new ideas, managing risk, and promoting a culture that embraces experimentation and continuous improvement.

8. Improving Decision-Making: Continuous learning improves critical thinking and problem-solving skills, helping bosses make more informed decisions. Training provides them with tools and frameworks to analyze complex situations, evaluate options, and consider different perspectives.

9. Developing Resilience: Training helps bosses build resilience and handle stress and challenges at work. It gives them strategies for self-care, maintaining work-life balance, and promoting well-being for themselves and their teams.

10. Modeling a Learning Culture: When leaders prioritize their own ongoing training, they set an example for their teams. This encourages a learning environment where employees are motivated to continually develop their skills and knowledge, building a more agile and innovative organization.

By understanding the importance of ongoing training and development, leaders can consistently improve their leadership skills, boost employee engagement, and adjust to the constantly changing demands of the business world.

Continuous Learning

In today's fast-changing business landscape, the importance of ongoing training and development for leaders cannot be overstated. A well-designed professional development program not only sharpens leadership skills but also promotes organizational success by fostering a culture of continuous learning and growth.

This initiative aims to provide leaders with the knowledge, skills, and tools needed to manage change, motivate employees, and effectively lead diverse and inclusive teams. By investing in their growth, leaders set the example for the entire organization, encouraging adaptability, innovation, and a dedication to excellence at every level.

Staying Current: Continuous training helps leaders keep up-to-date with the latest industry trends, best practices, and emerging technologies. This knowledge allows them to make informed decisions and guide their teams effectively in a quickly changing business environment. For example, leaders can attend industry conferences, join webinars, and subscribe to relevant publications to stay informed about new developments in their field.

Enhancing Leadership Skills: Training offers opportunities for leaders to improve their leadership abilities, including communication, conflict resolution, decision-making, and strategic thinking. These skills are vital for effective team management and organizational success. Leaders can participate in workshops, coaching sessions, and leadership development programs to sharpen their skills and learn new techniques.

Adapting to Change: Training gives leaders the skills to handle change and uncertainty. It helps them guide their teams through organizational shifts, adopt new technologies, and respond effectively to market changes. Leaders can engage in change management training, scenario planning exercises, and resilience activities to prepare for and manage change. Kotter's 8 steps might assist you in making a difference.

Fostering Employee Engagement: Leaders who invest in ongoing training show their commitment to employee growth and development. This encourages a culture of learning and engagement, boosting employee satisfaction and retention. Leaders can implement mentorship programs, facilitate team-building activities, and promote open communication to strengthen relationships with their teams.

Building Emotional Intelligence: Training in areas such as empathy, active listening, and relationship management helps leaders develop emotional intelligence. This skill is essential for effective leadership because it improves communication, collaboration, and employee motivation. Leaders can attend emotional intelligence workshops, practice reflection, and seek feedback to enhance their interpersonal skills.

Figure 2

Kotter's 8-Step Process for Leading Change includes the following steps:

1. **Establish a sense of urgency**: Highlight the importance of change to motivate stakeholders.
2. **Form a powerful coalition**: Assemble a group with enough power to lead the change.
3. **Create a vision for change**: Develop a clear vision to direct the change effort.
4. **Communicate the vision**: Share the vision with all stakeholders to gain support.
5. **Empower others to act on the vision**: Remove obstacles and enable people to contribute to the change.
6. **Create short-term wins**: Plan for visible improvements and celebrate them to build momentum.
7. **Consolidate gains and produce more change**: Use increased credibility to change systems, structures, and policies that don't fit the vision.
8. <u>**Anchor new approaches in the organization's culture: Ensure that the changes are seen in every aspect of the organization.**</u>

Managing Diversity and Inclusion: Ongoing training helps leaders develop the knowledge and skills needed to lead diverse and inclusive teams. It improves their cultural competence, reduces unconscious bias, and empowers them to create work environments where everyone feels valued and heard. Leaders can participate in diversity and inclusion training, engage with

Employee Resource Groups (ERGs) and the implementation of inclusive policies and practices.

Nurturing Innovation: Training encourages leaders to think creatively and fosters an environment that supports innovation. It gives them techniques for generating ideas, managing risks, and promoting a culture that welcomes experimentation and continuous improvement. Leaders can attend innovation workshops, collaborate with cross-functional teams, and create spaces for brainstorming and idea generation.

Improving Decision-Making: Ongoing learning encourages critical thinking and problem-solving abilities, helping leaders make better-informed decisions. Training provides them with the tools and frameworks needed to analyze complex situations, assess options, and consider diverse perspectives. Leaders can improve their decision-making skills by engaging in decision-making simulations, case studies, and peer learning.

Developing Resilience: Training helps leaders build resilience and handle stress and challenges at work. It provides them with strategies for self-care, maintaining work-life balance, and promoting well-being for themselves and their teams. Leaders can engage in resilience training, mindfulness practices, and wellness programs to improve their ability to thrive under pressure.

Modeling a Learning Culture: When leaders prioritize their ongoing training, they set an example for their teams. This fosters a learning culture where employees are encouraged to consistently develop their skills and knowledge, resulting in a more agile and innovative organization. Leaders can promote a learning culture by sharing their own learning experiences, encouraging curiosity, and providing access to learning resources.

By recognizing the importance of ongoing training and development, leaders can continuously improve their leadership skills, boost employee engagement, and adapt to the ever-changing demands of the business world. This professional growth process and program will empower leaders to lead with confidence, motivate their teams, and achieve long-term organizational success.

Critical Elements of Leadership Mastery

Leadership mastery is a complex journey that involves understanding and developing key elements essential for effective leadership. These elements cover various topics, each playing a crucial role in shaping a leader's ability to inspire, guide, and make a positive impact within an organization. Below is a comprehensive overview of these topics, along with relevant facts, citations, and websites.

1. Self-Awareness and Emotional Intelligence
    - Understanding one's strengths, weaknesses, and emotional triggers.
    - Developing empathy and the ability to manage emotions effectively.
2. Vision and Strategic Thinking
    - Creating a clear and compelling vision for the future.
    - Develop strategic plans to achieve organizational goals.
3. Communication Skills
    - Mastering the art of effective communication, both verbal and non-verbal.
    - Building strong relationships through active listening and clear messaging.

4. Decision-Making and Problem-Solving
    - Developing the ability to make informed and timely decisions.
    - Utilizing critical thinking and analytical skills to solve complex problems.
5. Team Building and Collaboration
    - Fostering a collaborative environment that encourages teamwork and innovation.
    - Building and leading diverse teams to achieve common goals.
6. Adaptability and Resilience
    - Embracing change and demonstrating resilience in the face of challenges.
    - Developing the ability to adapt to evolving circumstances and environments.

Leadership Development

The Center for Creative Leadership (CCL) has been a pioneer in leadership development for over 50 years. Their innovative techniques and models have significantly shaped the field, providing valuable insights into effective leadership practices.

1. Origins and Mission
    - Founded in 1970 with a mission to advance the understanding, practice, and development of leadership for the benefit of society worldwide.
2. Key Models and Frameworks
    - 70-20-10 Model: Emphasizes that 70% of learning comes from challenging assignments, 20% from developmental relationships, and 10% from formal training.

- SBI Model: Focuses on Situation-Behavior-Impact to provide clear and actionable feedback.
- Direction-Alignment-Commitment (DAC) Model: Highlights the importance of aligning team direction, fostering commitment, and ensuring alignment.

3. Innovative Programs

    - Leadership Development Program (LDP)®: The longest-running program of its kind, with over 100,000 alumni worldwide.
    - The Looking Glass Experience: A simulation that mimics the uncertain and ambiguous environment leaders face in the real world.

Preparing to Lead an Inclusive Organization

The qualities developed through leadership mastery are essential for leading an inclusive organization. Inclusive leadership involves creating an environment where all team members feel valued, respected, and empowered to contribute their unique perspectives. Here are some key qualities that prepare you to lead inclusively:

1. Visible Commitment

    - Demonstrating a genuine commitment to diversity and inclusion through actions and policies.

2. Humility

    - Acknowledging one's limitations and being open to learning from others3.

3. Awareness of Bias

- Recognizing and addressing unconscious biases that may affect decision-making3.

4. Curiosity About Others

    - Showing interest in understanding different perspectives and experiences3.

5. Cultural Intelligence

    - Developing the ability to interact effectively with people from diverse cultural backgrounds.

6. Effective Collaboration

    - Fostering a collaborative environment that leverages the strengths of diverse team members.

By mastering these elements, you can foster a more inclusive and dynamic organization that thrives on diversity and innovation. Such environments not only attract top talent but also enhance team collaboration, creativity, and long-term sustainability.

Chapter 4
Critical Thinking

"We are what we repeatedly do; excellence, then, is not an act but a habit."
–Aristotle

In growing older, we frequently encounter two phrases: "that's just common sense," and "that takes some critical thinking." Usually, we ignore them, but these phrases are significant. While we won't discuss common sense itself, we believe everyone either has it or doesn't. Instead, we'll focus on critical thinking. So, what exactly is it? Is it a way of approaching a problem from a specific perspective? Maybe, maybe not. In this chapter, we'll break it down into simpler parts to make it easier to understand. Critical thinking isn't just about finding answers; it's about asking the right questions. It challenges assumptions, sharpens judgment, and enables leaders to make informed, well-reasoned decisions under pressure.

As long as you don't deeply explore the meaning of critical thinking, you won't truly understand it. Some people believe that it is in our nature to act like critical thinkers whenever a complex situation arises. We fail to realize that our thinking is often biased and prejudiced, which is one of the most challenging and disruptive aspects of critical thinking. At the same time, we tend to overlook the simple fact that the quality of our lives heavily depends on our thinking patterns. Yes, this is a basic fact, but it is also incredibly concerning. Imagine building our lives on thinking patterns that are completely shortsighted and, to some extent, bigoted. Poor thinking, on the other hand, can be costly. Excellence in thought is vital, but it requires systematic effort over time. But the question remains: What is critical thinking?

A Critical mode of thinking

Critical thinking is a mode of thinking. In critical thinking, an individual examines a specific problem at hand and applies the inherent thinking structures along with some intellectual standards to it. These academic standards open the doors for greater discussion and reach a well-thought-out and neutral conclusion.

This is what a critical thinker does.
- Raises questions and shapes them very clearly.
- Gathers and evaluates relevant information and compares it against a specific standard or yardstick.
- It is critical, if not fundamental, to keep an open mind while keeping different scenarios in mind and thinking about practical consequences.
- Open, effective communication with all while coming up with the solution to a complex problem is always preferred.

To put it briefly, unlike conventional thinking, critical thinking is a well-directed, disciplined, and self-corrective mode of thinking, which opens up doors to better opportunities and possibilities. It also paves the way for better communication while enabling us to control our egocentrism.

Tools Of Critical Thinking

Now that we have discussed the definition of critical thinking and what exactly a critical thinker does, let's move forward and look at the essential tools of thinking. The following tools also play a role in this process:

Gathering Information

The first stage of critical thinking is collecting information.

Once you decide to develop effective strategies, you need to have the necessary and agreed-upon details ready.

Observation

Next, let's focus on observation. Suppose you've gathered all the necessary information. You will need to examine the details of what you've just collected more thoroughly.

Infer

Apply logic and come up with more options and possibilities.

Rationalization

Use reason to analyze an argument and evaluate the discussion to determine its strengths and weaknesses.

Reflection

Take a step back now and then, view the bigger picture, and recognize how far you've come.

Create

Use some creative thinking tools.

Classification and Sequencing

All items need to be organized and sorted based on their specific characteristics.

Compare-Contrast

After you realize how different one thing is from the other, you get to choose the one that best fits the criteria.

Cause and Effect

Examine the actions and their results to understand how they are linked.

Synthesize

Using the information you already have, generate some new outcomes.

Evaluate

Make a decision, evaluate it, and observe how it influences the final choice.

Predict

With the relevant information in hand, analyze current trends and predict what will happen in the future.

Prioritize

Assess the significance of any event or situation, then place it in proper perspective.

Summarize

Review all of your findings and then record all of your results.

Gathering Facts

You probably understood from the heading that it relates to gathering information. Yes, we'll talk about that in a moment. But before you go any further, it's important to realize that you shouldn't do this randomly or impulsively, like suddenly deciding to start critical thinking one day. You do it because you're looking for something. Something tangible that can actually improve your decision-making skills and help you make consistent choices in the future.

Speaking of decision-making, to make correct decisions, you need to be well-informed. In the fast-paced and competitive world we live in, managers and people in key roles must be very careful about their decisions, and once a decision is made, they should stand by it. However, before moving forward with a possible decision, you need to have the right information in hand.

In the medical field, I have seen nurses follow these steps as part of a patient care plan. They refer to it as SOAP.
S. (subject) O. (objective) A. (assessment) P. (plan). Here is
Another straightforward strategy to gather the much-needed data. Note the steps that will provide you with the information you need about a specific issue before you even consider reaching a conclusion.

Ask Some Simple Questions

- Do I have the right amount of information, or do I need some more?
- Is there some pattern of occurrences?
- Is the problem people-related or technology-related?
- Do I need to step outside the organization to gather information?
- Who are the people affected by a specific situation?

Talk with the Concerned People

Talking to people is beneficial for two reasons. First, it helps you gather the right amount of information. Second, it allows you to assist those facing specific dilemmas. Nine out of ten times, they will follow the course of action you recommend. There is a third reason: talking with your team gives you another chance to hear current "rumors," clarify your intent, correct misconceptions, and offer support as they work to implement change. Knowing the truth and seeing that the boss is actively addressing the issues can be a comfort.

Utilize the Available Resources

First, check the records in your library. They may also include information from vendors and suppliers. Then, talk to your manager and other employees. This will help you identify who has the right information and expertise, especially when an issue arises.

Organize Information

Organize the information you have collected carefully. Make sure to stay focused on your decision. Often, you'll notice a connection. Patterns will begin to emerge, and problems will become clearer, helping you to solve them.

Evaluate the Facts

Until now, we've talked about how to gather information, but the real work is still ahead. Imagine you've collected the information; now it's time to learn how to evaluate it. So, let's get started.

Currency

When it comes to the timelessness of information, you need to ask some critical questions.

- When was it published? Remember, some older publications are classics.
- Has it ever been updated or revised?
- Do we need more information and are the available links still functional?

Relevance

- Is the information relevant and does it answer your question?
- Who is the information actually for and who is the intended audience?

- Is it on an appropriate level?
- Is it understood?
- Are there other various information sources available or is this the only one?
- Can we site this source?

AUthority

- Who is the information coming from?
- What are the credentials of the person or the organization that the information is coming from?
- Is the person qualified to present us with this piece of information?
- Are there contact details for the verification of the information that we have just landed?

AccUracy

- Is there sufficient evidence to back this information that we have just gathered?
- Has it ever been reviewed or referred to in the past?
- Can it be verified through personal knowledge or another credible source?
- Does the tone seem unbiased and impartial?
- Are there any errors in the facts we have gathered?

PUrpoSe

- What is the purpose of the information at hand?
- Does it exist to persuade, sell, entertain, or teach?
- Is it information/fact or just propaganda or opinion?
- Is the viewpoint objective and impartial?
- Are there any political, ideological, or personal biases involved with the information?

Reaching Conclusions using Logic

After gathering and evaluating the necessary information for your critical thinking, you must reach a logical conclusion. A logical conclusion may seem right to most people, but this is not always the case. In the next section, we will examine some of the most common types of logic and how they influence your conclusions. Understanding these types helps you recognize flawed reasoning, strengthen your arguments, and ensure that decisions are based on clear, rational foundations rather than assumptions or emotions.

Formal Logic

First on our list is formal logic. In this form of logic, we use deductive reasoning, and the premises should always be true. The premises are then used to reach a formal conclusion.

Symbolic Logic

As the name suggests, in symbolic knowledge, we understand how symbols relate to each other. This form of reasoning involves assigning symbols in verbal reasoning to verify the truth of statements in a mathematical process. This type of logic is mostly used in calculus.

Informal Logic

This is the logic we use in daily reasoning. It involves the arguments and reasoning you use in your interactions with those around you.

Mathematical Knowledge

In this form of logic, formal logic is applied to mathematics. This type of knowledge serves as part of the basis for reasoning used in computer science. Often, mathematical reasoning and symbols are used interchangeably.

Evaluation of Big Decisions

If you can remember, at the beginning, we discussed decision-making, and in fact, it is the decision that is the final result of the critical thinking process. However, after you conclude, you then need to evaluate it. But how can we evaluate our decisions? For the practical evaluation of findings, here are a few questions that need to be asked.

What Is the Significance of This Decision?

With time, a big decision needs deliberation. Well, this question is only partially complete. The other half of the problem is, "What are the costs of failing to do what we have proposed to do?" Revisiting your decisions is beneficial, as it allows you to refine what you initially set out to do. It is because of sound decisions that the mission of an organization is affirmed.

Who Is It That Benefits from the Decision?

A decision leads to change, and when there is change, some will lose, while others will emerge victorious. It means that some may gain power, while others will only lose it. Then there will be those who suffer in some form of inconvenience. One thing that you cannot avoid is severe resentment and resistance towards the new decision. This is where management and leadership skills are put to the test. If you are the person in charge, you will have to make sure that everyone makes the most out of the new decision. If there are any grievances, you will have to learn to handle them.

What If the Decision Is Reversed?

When it comes to reversing a decision, some costs need

to be paid. Most of all, by changing a decision, you waste significant resources such as time and money. Such U-turns can make your company appear haphazard and unfocused. However, at the same time, you can also save time and money by involving stakeholders.

What's Best for the Organization?

Leaders face several challenges daily. But why does it happen? It happens only because the organization asks them to do so. When a decision proves bad, it seems wise to hold the course. But why? Because the long-term pain is far deadlier, especially when it is compared to short-term gains. In big corporate organizations, this is quite common.

Unconscious Bias

Before moving toward unconscious bias, you need to understand what a bias is. Bias is usually a prejudice against or for a particular person, thing, idea, or group of people, which could be unfair. All of us tend to have certain biases that can have negative or positive effects, depending on the situation.

There are mainly two types of biases: conscious and unconscious biases. These biases are not limited to someone's race or ethnicity. Although racial and ethnic biases are well documented, biases against other groups also exist. A person's age, gender, religion, disabilities, appearance, sexual orientation, and even personal likes and dislikes can be subject to bias. An unconscious bias is a prejudice directed at a specific person or group, often in the form of stereotypes that exist outside of their awareness.

Every person has specific views about certain social and identity groups, and these biases influence how they relate to these groups. Unlike conscious prejudice, unconscious biases are more common and often conflict with a person's conscious beliefs. Situations like working under high pressure with many people can easily trigger these unconscious biases.

Micro-Aggressions

Simply put, a micro-aggression is verbal or non-verbal behavior that happens consciously or unconsciously and targets a member of a marginalized group, such as an ethnic, religious, or gender minority. It often has a harmful or derogatory impact.

Types of Micro-Aggression

Some of the most common types of micro aggressions are as follows:

Micro assaults: These are intentional acts, and the person committing them is aware they are harmful.

Micro Insult: They are more subtle. Usually, they are slurs with a hidden meaning.

Micro Invalidation: It is more like gas lighting. It is just like telling a person from an ethnic or religious minority that their emotions are invalid, and they are overreacting towards an insult or slur that doesn't seem too significant to the person coming up with the micro invalidation. It may often lead to abuse or insult, like the ones mentioned above.

Environmental Micro-aggressions: Things in our environment or the media that send a message of invalidation for a somewhat marginalized group.

Some Common Examples of Micro-Aggression

- A female health professional enters a room. We think she is a nurse and not a doctor.
- A person meets another person of Asian ancestry and asks where they are from.
- You avoid someone on purpose just because they look a certain way.
- Telling a member of the LGBT community that they

don't seem too "gay."
- A woman is told that she is bossy because she voiced her opinion during a meeting.
- A member of a visible minority is told that they are very articulate.

Chapter 5
Role of I&I Professionals in Facilitating Change

"Understand that commitment to a major change is always expensive and that you either pay for achieving it or pay for not having it."

—*Daryl Conner*

Understanding I&I Professionals

Innovation and inclusion (I & I) is a relatively new concept that draws strength from the reality of creative forces when they come together. This combination occurs not only when humans blend their physical and mental energies to solve problems but also in the unique way they employ tools to tackle new and different challenges in both corporate offices and the field.

I&I is based on the old philosophy that we can accomplish more together when we collaborate. This concept originated from the author's experience working with NASA. I&I has become a strategy that most leading organizations have adopted. Effective I&I strategies go beyond previous brainstorming techniques to drive positive change, foster innovation, and build a culture of inclusion and continuous learning. It is no surprise that humanity would not be where it is today without the coming together of people who had a different approach to reading a situation and thus overcoming their shortcomings. These strategies are no longer optional; they are vital for companies that want to stay competitive and relevant in a diverse global market.

According to the Institute for Diversity Certification (IDC), the DEI process can improve your business through I&I strategies. The best advice comes from I&I professionals. These experts are essential in creating workplaces where diverse perspectives are valued and all employees have equal chances to succeed.

This chapter explores the role of I&I professionals, their responsibilities, and the valuable contributions they bring to organizations. We will also discuss how to work effectively with these professionals to develop and implement I&I strategies and how to empower them to become agents of meaningful change.

As technology advances, the world has become a global village. Consequently, the workforce in companies is diverse and comes from various social and cultural backgrounds. When managing a diverse workforce, it is crucial to ensure that all team members are aligned, despite their artistic and social differences. Achieving this cohesion can be difficult, but I&I professionals provide invaluable expertise in bridging these gaps.

These professionals play a vital role, from implementing policies that promote innovation and inclusion in the workplace to developing roadmaps for the company's success while maintaining a diverse and inclusive workforce. The changing role of I&I professionals in the organizational landscape makes them essential for both emerging and established businesses. Their positions include diversity officers, inclusion managers, and equity strategists. However, their expertise and guidance can drive a company toward success, boost productivity, and foster a work environment founded on the principles of innovation and inclusion.

Value Proposition of I&I Professionals

I&I professionals are strategic partners who can enhance your business and work environment. They positively influence organizational success by fostering cohesion among a diverse workforce and actively helping to create a psychologically safe and barrier-free workplace.

Partnering with I&I professionals can add value to your business in the following ways:

Inclusive Leadership Framework: Inclusive leadership is a fundamental component of I&I initiatives. These leaders ensure their teams have a clear purpose, defined processes, and well-established roles. They also cultivate an environment where diversity is celebrated and integrated into innovative ways of thinking, designing, and acting. I&I professionals can assist in creating a framework that encourages leadership behaviors and promotes inclusivity. This framework includes developing a clear vision for organizational success, designing and implementing leadership training programs, and establishing accountability measures to support inclusive leadership.

Diversity Training Programs: Diversity training is essential for organizations with varied workforces. It helps overcome implicit bias and fosters a psychologically safe environment for everyone. I&I professionals create content and lead these training sessions. Their experience and guidance ensure the programs are both informative and transformative, promoting lasting change in organizational culture and practices.

Tailoring Initiatives and Knowledge Management: I&I professionals develop customized roadmaps for implementing essential initiatives, set measurable goals and milestones, propose design interventions that address specific organizational needs, and align I&I strategies with overall business objectives. Knowledge management is also vital for driving change, and these professionals incorporate it into their comprehensive vision for an innovative and inclusive work environment.

Assessment Techniques: These professionals also measure impact through ROI (Return on Investment), demonstrating the value of I&I initiatives. This includes establishing key performance indicators (KPIs), collecting and analyzing data, reporting outcomes to leadership and stakeholders, and using insights to refine and improve future strategies.

Ensuring Compliance and Ethical Standards: Quality and standards assurance are essential to this role. I&I professionals stay informed about relevant laws and regulations, develop and enforce policies that support I&I goals, address ethical dilemmas related to potential initiatives, and promote transparency in decision-making processes.

Building Effective I&I Strategies

These professionals can create effective I&I strategies tailored to your business and leadership objectives. Some methods that I&I professionals can implement are discussed below.

Aligning I&I with Organizational Goals

The primary strategy is to align the organization's goals with the core principles of innovation and inclusion. Ensure that every aspect of the organization, from hiring and management to execution, is free of bias and inclusive. Promoting open communication is also crucial. Once these principles are aligned with the company's objectives, implementing I&I strategies will become much easier.

Developing a Comprehensive I&I Framework

These professionals develop a comprehensive framework that addresses all aspects of I&I within the organization, including policies, practices, and programs that promote a culture of creativity and belonging. Their goals often include forming cross-functional teams to lead I&I initiatives, setting clear accountability measures, and creating ongoing feedback and improvement systems.

Leveraging Data and Analytics for I&I Initiatives

No strategy can succeed without proper measurement and analysis to track impact and outcomes. I&I professionals can lead in this area by conducting regular diversity audits, analyzing employee engagement surveys, or using predictive analytics to identify potential exclusion zones or risks to the work environment. They can establish clear KPIs (key performance indicators) and consistently report progress to stakeholders. By utilizing advanced analytics, I&I professionals enable organizations to make informed decisions based on reliable data.

Change Management

The only thing that remains constant in our professional and personal lives is change. One term that gets tossed around more often is change management. So, what is change management, which has been a heated discussion topic for quite some time? Let's find out.

Change management is a discipline that helps guide, support, and equip individuals with the skills and information they need to embrace changes that improve the company. For the company to succeed and achieve greater success than before, it must continue to evolve, which means effectively managing change.

So, what are the reasons for change management within an organization? Let's break it down:

- It creates an attractive and fulfilling workplace.
- It adds to the overall experience of the employees in the organization.
- It decreases costs on projects and ensures the desired results.
- It minimizes employee resistance, and at the same time, it increases employee satisfaction.

Increases profitability:

- It enables you to provide an enhanced customer experience.
- It helps you cultivate the desired workplace culture.
- It ensures technological advancement within the organization.
- It provides you with more realistic and futuristic training solutions.
- An organizational strategy that is far more relevant to the current situation and the ever-changing circumstances.

- It ensures alignment between change projects and organizational strategy.

Some of the barriers to change management are as follows:

- Lack of understanding regarding change and its impacts
- Change can have a negative impact on the employees.
- Poor communication
- Inability to involve employees in the change processes
- Lack of budget and resources

There frequently is resistance to the cultural shift in the organization.

- The management isn't incredibly supportive of change.
- No commitment to change
- The influence of past trauma of failed change initiatives

Here are some of the consequences of poor change management.

- Financial loss
- Decline in productivity
- The quality of work tends to suffer
- Time and other vital resources get wasted.
- Low staff morale
- Poor employee retention
- Spike in employee sickness
- Reduction inefficiency of the team
- Negative impact on customers, suppliers, and vendors
- Missed chances of growth

Ways to Ensure Effective Change Management

Here are some of the ways to ensure effective change management in an organization.

- Define very clearly what change means to you and align it with your business goals.
- Determine the impacts of your initiatives and the people and the things that will be affected.

Develop a comprehensive communication strategy.

- Provide practical and relevant training to your team members. Introduce and implement a support structure.
- Measure the change process with the standards and the goals that you had in mind in the beginning.

Engaging and Empowering I&I Professionals

Effective engagement and empowerment of I&I professionals are essential for driving significant change within organizations. However, the roles of these professionals are often undervalued, leading to their services being overlooked. As a CEO, you must avoid this mistake and recognize the value of integrating I&I professionals into your firm.

I&I professionals can be empowered and encouraged to contribute to the organizational success through the following ways:

Creating an Inclusive I&I Culture: The first step toward engaging and empowering I&I professionals is to provide an environment where they feel valued and heard. Integrating I&I principles into the company's core values and decision-making processes, actively seeking input from I&I professionals on strategic issues, and visibly supporting their initiatives can help foster a culture of transparency and inclusion. Regular meetings, feedback sessions, and open-door policies can also contribute.

Development Opportunities for I&I Professionals: Companies should emphasize continuous learning and growth for I&I professionals to stay competitive. Creating a dedicated career path for I&I specialists can also help retain talented staff and show the firm's ongoing commitment to this area. Additionally, organizations can assist I&I professionals in earning relevant certifications or advanced degrees to boost their expertise.

Cross-functional Collaboration: Innovation and inclusion strategies should not operate in isolation. Collaboration among professionals from different departments can lead to a more comprehensive and effective strategy. This may include forming multi-disciplinary teams to address specific issues or integrating I&I experts into product development groups for inclusive design. Regular inter-departmental meetings help professionals understand diverse business needs and adjust their approaches accordingly. Such collaboration also promotes the spread of I&I principles throughout the organization instead of treating them as separate initiatives.

Fostering Innovation Through Employee Empowerment: Just as you aim to empower your employees through I&I strategies, you should also consider the professionals responsible for developing these strategies. Make sure they are empowered to make decisions, share their ideas, and feel a sense of belonging within your company, which encourages them to give their best to the organization. By promoting a culture where every employee feels empowered to contribute ideas, organizations can access a diverse range of creativity and foster meaningful innovation.

I&I Professionals as Change Agents

Professionals act as catalysts for positive change, transforming entire organizations. Their unique roles enable them to impact organizational culture, practices, and strategies.

The multiple roles played by these professionals as agents of change are as follows:

Overcoming Challenges: I&I professionals face many obstacles in their change efforts, including resistance to change, implicit biases, and resource limitations. They address these challenges by developing communication strategies, forming strong coalitions, and presenting compelling business cases for I&I initiatives. By anticipating obstacles and creating effective mitigation plans, they can successfully navigate complex organizational dynamics and drive meaningful change.

Building a Change-Ready Organization: Another responsibility of I&I professionals is cultivating an organizational culture open to change. They start by promoting a growth mindset across the organization, encouraging calculated risk-taking, and fostering adaptability. They focus on equipping leaders and employees with skills to handle transitions successfully. I&I professionals assist organizations in becoming more responsive to emerging trends by implementing clear change management processes and establishing effective feedback mechanisms.

Sustaining I&I Momentum: Maintaining a long-term commitment to I&I initiatives is crucial for creating a lasting impact. I&I professionals achieve this by consistently demonstrating the value of innovation and inclusive efforts, celebrating successes, and learning from setbacks. They establish systems for ongoing measurement and progress reporting, ensuring risks remain a priority for the organization. They build a distributed change leadership model by cultivating a network of I&I champions across various departments and levels.

Conclusion

I&I professionals play a vital role in driving change, from creating comprehensive strategies to assessing their impact and results. These professionals overcome challenges, cultivate inclusive cultures, and encourage innovation through employee empowerment, making them essential to the organization.

As businesses navigate quickly changing markets and shifting consumer expectations, the ability to innovate and be inclusive will be a key advantage for those seeking to succeed. I&I professionals will lead this transformation, guiding organizations through obstacles and helping them keep up with new trends.

Part II
Multiple Management Perspectives

Chapter 6
Understanding Power Dynamics and Privilege

"Leadership is not about titles, positions, or flow charts. It is about one life influencing another."

—*John C. Maxwell*

Power dynamics and privilege have been present throughout various stages of life, from workplaces to community spaces. We first encounter these power dynamics early on, in playgrounds and schools. Bullying is a common form of abuse of power within these contexts. As we grow older, we also see these dynamics play out in our workplaces.

History shows how privilege exists and harms people over time. Whether it's male privilege or White privilege, there's always a group that gets more advantages. As a result, the other group often feels oppressed because of unfair working or living conditions.

Organizations risk missing out on innovative ideas and diverse perspectives when they fail to address power imbalances and privilege. Therefore, understanding power dynamics and privilege is crucial for managing a workplace effectively. These power structures, if left unchecked, create invisible barriers that hinder collaboration, reduce morale, and limit upward mobility for underrepresented groups. Addressing these issues requires a proactive approach through inclusive policies, equitable leadership development, and the creation of safe spaces for dialogue. By empowering employees from all backgrounds and ensuring accountability at every level, organizations can build a culture of respect and shared responsibility, which in turn promotes long-term success.

Power Dynamics in Organizations

Power dynamics refer to the inherent structures and influences of power between individuals and groups within a specific setting. In a workplace, power dynamics describe the relationship between employees and supervisors or the workforce and their leaders. It can also refer to the hierarchy of power from the top, such as the CEO, to managers and then to staff.[1]

Different types of power exist in the workplace, including positional, personal, and social capital. Positional power is the authority held by individuals in higher roles over their subordinates. Personal power refers to how employees use their connections and relationships to influence others. Social capital provides financial power, often used in business partnerships where a more financially stable partner makes key decisions, while the other partners may contribute less.

Power dynamics affect us in many ways. They can shape decision-making, promotions, and access to resources. Therefore, understanding the current power dynamics in an organization is crucial for navigating them effectively and reducing their harmful effects.

Understanding Privilege

According to social thinker Allan G. Johnson, privilege refers to any unearned, exclusive, and socially granted advantage. This privilege can be gained from belonging to a particular race, gender, or class. Therefore, the advantage given to certain people because of their social identity is called privilege.

People who benefit from social privilege are often unaware of it, accepting the advantages without recognizing their source. Throughout history, we have seen many examples of privilege and its harmful effects on society. White privilege contributed to apartheid, male privilege led to female workers demanding equal pay, and class privilege sparked revolts and the overthrow of governments by ordinary people, like during the French Revolution.

However, privilege persists even in today's advanced society. Despite all the education and technology, humans have not been able to eliminate the social norms that have been ingrained in human life for a long time. Therefore, privilege can appear in the workplace through microaggressions, unconscious bias, and lack of representation.

Power dynamics in supervisor-employee relationships are complex and can influence many aspects of how an organization functions. When used unfairly, they can hinder the organization's progress and growth.

The Adverse Impact Of Power Imbalance

Decision-Making: Power dynamics can influence hiring, promotion, and resource allocation decisions. Individuals who hold power and privilege in an organization (such as those in managerial positions) might abuse their power to make biased decisions. For example, hiring a candidate based on association instead of merit demonstrates the unfair use of power by the recruiter. This selected candidate may not be the best fit for the job, but they were chosen for reasons such as impressing the recruiter or other factors that led to their selection over other candidates. Therefore, the decision-making process is impacted, which can jeopardize the company's future sooner or later.

Workplace Culture: Abuse of power and unfair privileges can create an environment of exclusion or silence. Employees feel oppressed and hesitate to speak out against those who hold authority and benefits within their organization. This fosters resentment and hampers their performance, as they believe their company does not value them.

Microaggressions and Unconscious Bias: The subtle ways that power dynamics and privilege influence daily interactions can lead to microaggressions. Unconscious bias by those in influential roles within a firm creates a deep division among employees, which can impact performance, hinder inclusivity, and cause resentment that manifests as arguments and aggression.

Limited Opportunities: Privilege can create barriers to advancement for marginalized groups. A relevant example is the unequal pay for men and women in several industries. Male privilege may also increase male employees' chances of promotion to managerial roles ahead of females.

Employee Engagement: Unchecked power and unacknowledged privilege can affect employee morale and engagement. When people feel unheard and unvalued in a working environment, they refrain from engaging positively, which might also affect their performance. People are happy to work for organizations that make them feel valued and appreciate their efforts. In a workplace where their efforts go unacknowledged, they tend to stop contributing altogether, affecting the overall progress of the firm.

Tips and Tricks for Navigating Power Dynamics

Power exists in every workplace, but it is important to recognize that it can have both positive and negative effects. Using power dynamics constructively can bring many benefits to your organization and its employees. Conducting surveys, focus groups, and employee interviews can help you understand power and privilege in the workplace from their perspective and take appropriate actions.

You can exercise your power positively and facilitate your employees in the following ways:

Innovation and Inclusion (I&I) Training: Creating awareness and providing training for leadership and employees is essential to building an inclusive and equitable workforce culture. Arrange coaching programs that make your employees aware of the benefits of being innovative and inclusive, allowing them equal opportunities to contribute and learn from their peers. You can also establish a reward system for employees who complete this training and implement it professionally.

Structured Hiring and Promotion Processes: Using objective criteria to reduce bias in decision-making can also balance power and eliminate unfair privilege. Transparent promotions are an effective way to ensure workplace equity by advancing employees based on their performance and merit. Likewise, implementing a structured hiring process where candidates are tested for their abilities and selected can drive the company's growth and success while preventing implicit bias in decision-making.

Mentorship Programs: Establishing mentorship programs creates opportunities for underrepresented groups and helps them feel empowered and valued by their firm. Start at the lowest level of your company (such as interns and technical workers), assigning them to experienced employees who are willing to coach and showcase their abilities positively. This process encourages workplace learning, and by involving employees from different levels, you can foster understanding and a culture of shared respect.

Employee Resource Groups (ERGs): Supporting the development of ERGs promotes inclusivity and a sense of belonging. Establish resource groups for your employees that address their needs and provide support. These groups become a reliable place your employees can turn to whenever they need help, support, guidance, or any other resources their companies offer.

Open Communication and Feedback: Building trust and encouraging open dialogue about experiences with power dynamics and privilege can help address power imbalances and enhance workplace culture. Foster an environment where all employees feel comfortable sharing their ideas and communicating with each other without any status barriers. Providing meaningful feedback on their ideas will motivate them to express themselves and learn at the same time.

Flexible Working Arrangements: Family-friendly policies and flexible work setups motivate people to work harder and do their best. It is a myth that flexible working hinders productivity. It often allows employees to work at their own pace and promotes a culture of respect and mutual growth. It also boosts your company's overall employee retention and satisfaction.

Building a More Equitable Workplace

An equitable workplace can only be created when all employees feel valued and appreciated, regardless of race, social class, or gender. Their performance should be the only criterion for qualifying for their positions, encouraging them to do their best in every situation. Bringing together diverse individuals and uniting them under your company's roof will only be beneficial if you address their needs, make them feel valued by the company, and foster a friendly relationship between employees and leaders. As Desmond Tutu famously said, "Differences are not intended to separate, to alienate. We are different precisely to realize our need for one another."

As a leader and CEO of your company, your response to power dynamics and privilege is very important. If you create a workplace where the main focus isn't on having power but on respecting people and working together as a team, you'll notice the difference in how your employees contribute to your vision. Remember, you need to lead by example, and only then will your employees follow your lead. Hierarchies are necessary in the workplace, but encouraging everyone to treat each other with respect, no matter their position, helps create an environment free of politics, privilege, and abuse of power.

Impact of power dynamics and privilege in workplaces

Some questions for introspection that can help you understand the power dynamics of your company are stated below.

1. Who holds formal decision-making authority within the company?
2. How are promotions and raises typically decided?
3. Do certain departments or teams have more influence than others?
4. Are there social groups or cliques in your company that hold informal power?
5. Do employees feel comfortable expressing their ideas and opinions, regardless of background or position?
6. Are there opportunities for professional development available to all employees?
7. Is there a sense of fairness and respect in how employees are treated?
8. Does the company leadership reflect the diversity of the workforce?
9. How are company policies and decisions communicated to employees?
10. Do all employees, regardless of level, have access to the same information?

Reflecting on these questions and coming up with the answers will help you better understand the workplace environment you are currently providing to your employees. Furthermore, it will help you develop strategies to build a more equitable workplace.

Case Study — Marc Benioff, Salesforce

Marc Benioff founded Salesforce in 1999 and led it to success by focusing on employee and customer-friendly strategies. He promoted social and environmental causes, incorporating these values into the company culture and attracting like-minded employees. Benioff pledged 1% of the company's equity, products, and employee time to the community, a movement adopted by many reputable companies. He developed strong relationships with key stakeholders, including customers, partners, and employees. Under his leadership, Salesforce became the world's third-largest enterprise software company and a Fortune 150 firm with over 70,000 employees. Benioff has received numerous awards, including the prestigious 'Chevalier de la Légion d'honneur' from France.

Conclusion

Recognizing and addressing power dynamics and privilege is essential for achieving a truly inclusive and equitable workplace. As a CEO, you are responsible for ensuring a conducive and inclusive environment for all your employees.

Promoting I&I in the workplace is the best way to foster a culture of fairness and respect for everyone. Supporting your employees through resource groups, mentorship programs, open communication, and feedback will create an equitable workforce where all feel welcome and appreciated.

As a leader, you must unite everyone in your organization, fostering a connection that creates a strong team beyond politics of power and privilege. Every employee is equally important, and by recognizing their contributions and offering your support, you can build trust in both you and the company. As a result, they will feel empowered to work with you and perform at their highest potential.

Chapter 7
Engaging Employee Resource Groups (ERGs) and Allies

"Unity in diversity is our strength."
--- José Bolton Sr., Ph.D.

Employee Resource Groups (ERGs)

Employee Resource Groups, also known as Affinity Groups or Employee Networks, are voluntary employee-led organizations that bring together individuals who share common backgrounds, experiences, or identities. ERGs offer a platform for employees to connect, support each other, and promote inclusivity within the organization. They serve as important resources for networking, mentoring, professional growth, and advancing I & I initiatives. The steps involved in establishing ERGs typically include:

  a. Establishing Purpose and Scope: Clearly define the purpose and scope of each ERG, specifying the particular affinity or focus area it represents. Examples include groups for women, LGBTQ+ employees, racial/ethnic minorities, veterans, or employees with disabilities1.

  b. Building Support and Leadership: Gain backing from executive sponsors and senior leaders who champion the ERGs. Appoint ERG leaders or steering committees responsible for guiding the group's activities, fostering engagement, and aligning their efforts with the organization's I & I goals1.

  c. Recruitment and Membership: Promote ERGs across the organization and encourage employees to join groups that match their identities or interests. Establish clear membership criteria and ensure accessibility and inclusivity for all employees interested in participating.

d. Establishing Governance and Structure: Define the governance framework for the ERGs, including roles and responsibilities, decision-making procedures, and alignment with the organization's policies and procedures. This ensures that ERGs function within the organization's framework while maintaining their independence.

e. Programming and Activities: Assist ERGs in planning and executing various activities, such as networking events, guest speaker sessions, professional development workshops, cultural celebrations, community outreach, and initiatives that support the organization's I & I goals.

Allies

Allies are people who actively support and advocate for members of marginalized or underrepresented groups, even if they are not part of those groups themselves. Allies use their privilege and influence to foster inclusive environments and challenge biases and discrimination. The stages of engaging allies typically include:

a. Education and Awareness: Offer educational resources, workshops, and training sessions to help employees understand the concept of allyship, recognize their privilege, and develop the skills needed to be effective allies.

b. Creating an Ally Network: Develop a platform or network where employees interested in becoming allies can connect, share resources, and work together on initiatives that promote inclusion and equity within the organization.

c. Encouraging Dialogue and Listening: Promote open and honest conversations where allies actively listen to the experiences, concerns, and perspectives of marginalized groups. This helps allies gain deeper insights and guides their actions and advocacy1.

d. Amplifying Marginalized Voices: Allies leverage their influence and privilege to elevate the voices of marginalized groups and advocate for their needs and rights. They actively support and promote the initiatives and activities of ERGs1.

e. Continuous Learning and Growth: Encourage allies to educate themselves on I & I topics consistently, stay updated on current issues and best practices, and challenge their own biases. Offer ongoing learning opportunities to support their growth and development as effective allies.

Summary: Engaging Employee Resource Groups (ERGs) and Allies is a powerful way to promote I & I within an organization. ERGs are voluntary, employee-led groups that unite individuals with common backgrounds, experiences, or identities. They offer a platform for employees to connect, support each other, and advocate for inclusivity. The stages of implementing ERGs typically include defining purpose and scope, building support and leadership, recruiting members, establishing governance and structure, and planning programs and activities. Allies are individuals who actively support and advocate for members of marginalized or underrepresented groups. Engaging allies generally involves education and awareness, creating an ally network, encouraging dialogue and listening, amplifying marginalized voices, and ongoing learning and growth. By following these stages for ERGs and engaging allies, organizations can create a more inclusive and supportive environment where I & I initiatives permeate all aspects of the organization, leading to improved employee engagement, retention, and overall success.

This report offers a comprehensive guide on developing inclusive leadership skills and engaging Employee Resource Groups (ERGs) and allies to support Inclusion & Innovation (I & I) within organizations. It emphasizes the role of ERGs in building community and fostering a sense of belonging, providing advice on creating and supporting ERGs as platforms for networking, advocacy, and advancing I & I initiatives.

By implementing these stages for ERGs and engaging allies, organizations can create a more inclusive and supportive environment where I & I initiatives influence all parts of the organization, leading to improved employee engagement, retention, and overall success.

Sure, let's look at an example of an Employee Resource Group (ERG) and track its development from individual interest to a fully established organization. We will also briefly explain how it differs from a Business Resource Group (BRG).

Example of ERG Development

Individual Interest: Imagine an employee named Alex who is passionate about supporting LGBTQ+ colleagues in the workplace. Alex notices that there is a lack of resources and support for LGBTQ+ employees and decides to take action. Alex begins by discussing the idea with a few colleagues who share the same interests and concerns.

Formation of ERG: Alex and interested colleagues decide to form an LGBTQ+ Employee Resource Group (ERG). They start by defining the purpose and scope of the ERG, which includes creating a safe space for LGBTQ+ employees, advocating for inclusive policies, and organizing events to raise awareness about LGBTQ+ issues.

Building Support and Leadership: The group seeks backing from executive sponsors and senior leaders who champion the ERG. They designate ERG leaders or a steering committee responsible for guiding the group's activities, fostering engagement, and aligning their efforts with the organization's Inclusion & Innovation (I & I) goals.

Recruitment and Membership: The ERG promotes its mission across the organization and encourages employees to join. They establish clear membership criteria and ensure accessibility and inclusivity for all employees who want to participate.

Establishing Governance and Structure: The ERG defines its governance framework, including roles and responsibilities, decision-making procedures, and alignment with the organization's policies and procedures. This ensures that the ERG functions within the organization's framework while maintaining its independence.

Programming and Activities: The ERG plans and carries out a variety of activities, including networking events, guest speaker sessions, professional development workshops, cultural celebrations, community outreach, and initiatives that support the organization's I & I goals.

Difference between ERG and BRG

Employee Resource Groups (ERGs): ERGs are voluntary, employee-led organizations that unite individuals who share common backgrounds, experiences, or identities. They aim to provide support, networking opportunities, mentoring, and advocacy to promote inclusivity within the organization. ERGs mainly focus on personal and social identities, such as race, gender, sexual orientation, or disability.

Business Resource Groups (BRGs): BRGs are also employee-led groups, but they focus on advancing business objectives and results. Although they share some traits with ERGs, BRGs are more closely aligned with the organization's strategic goals and often work on initiatives that directly influence the business, such as market research, product development, and customer engagement. BRGs utilize the diverse perspectives and expertise of their members to help the organization succeed.

In summary, while ERGs focus on creating a supportive and inclusive environment for employees based on shared identities, BRGs are more business-oriented and aim to drive organizational goals and outcomes through the diverse insights and contributions of their members.

Part III
Dynamic Business Environment

Chapter 8
Culture

"The culture of any organization is shaped by the worst behavior the leader is willing to tolerate."
—Gruenert and Whitaker

Today's workplace faces many challenges. Employees are expected to do more with less, even though they have access to nearly everything in the twenty-first century. Incidents related to workplace health are rising, and reports of workplace violence are increasing. Additionally, staff burnout is at an all-time high. Then COVID-19 arrived like the cherry on top; it dramatically changed the work environment and decreased coworker comfort.

Many aspects need to be redefined to reflect what the Earth has experienced over the past two years, now that life has returned to what could be called the new normal. The impacts of the pandemic are still felt in the workplace today, and it is often reported that businesses are implementing measures to change their culture with independent, unbiased, neutral, confidential, and informal resources.

Initiatives, listening sessions, and restructuring plans are frequently included. However, none effectively address the core issue, and it eventually reemerges. The truth is, employees are unhappy with how things are managed at work. But why? The workplace culture is the key to solving these problems. Culture shapes employees' daily experiences, affecting their motivation, well-being, and sense of belonging. Without a healthy, supportive culture that promotes transparency, respect, and flexibility, even the best policies and programs will fall short. To truly transform the workplace, organizations must focus on creating an environment where employees feel heard, valued, and empowered to succeed. This cultural shift is no longer optional—it's essential for long-term success.

The key to resolving workplace issues is organizational culture. Culture is defined as the unwritten social framework of an organization. It is responsible for permanently transforming attitudes and behaviors in these areas.

The Defense Equal Opportunity Management Institute (DEOMI) stands as a leader in innovation and inclusion within the U.S. Armed Forces. Previously, they have discussed the organization's culture regarding both individual and organizational change. The success or failure of an organization and its managers is often predicted by its culture. This chapter on culture explores the concepts of personal and organizational culture, how they develop, and the importance of recognizing and considering them when developing strategies to run an inclusive organization.

What is discouraged, encouraged, rejected, or accepted in a group depends on the cultural norms of the organization. An organizational culture can generate remarkable energy toward a shared purpose when it properly aligns with individual beliefs, needs, and motivations. Additionally, it fosters an environment that enables businesses to thrive. [1]

The Center for Advanced Research on Language Acquisition further defines culture as shared patterns of behaviors, interactions, cognitive constructs, and understanding learned through socialization. [2] Thus, culture can be seen as the development of a group identity fostered by social patterns unique to that group.

According to Edgar Schein, there are four categories of culture:

- Macro-cultures
- Organizational cultures
- Subcultures
- Micro-cultures

Macro-cultures consist of religious and ethnic groups, occupations, and nations worldwide. Although macro-culture encompasses a broad part of the world, our focus is on organizational culture, which includes all government, non-profit, public, and private organizations.

Subcultures include occupational and organizational groups, while micro cultures encompass all the microsystems within and outside an organization.

Organizational Cultures and Values

Managers often talk about building the 'right type of culture' or mention actions like 'fostering a culture of quality,' suggesting that an organization's culture depends on the values upper management wants to create.

Additionally, the way managers use the term 'culture' implies that some cultures are worse or weaker than others, and that fostering the 'right' culture can greatly influence an organization's effectiveness. In management literature, it is often suggested that having the right culture is crucial for effective performance, and a stronger culture is seen as directly linked to an organization's success. [3]

Researchers worldwide support these implications, as findings have shown that various cultural dimensions do, in fact, correlate with economic performance. However, a limiting factor of the entire premise arises from the existence of a wide range of organizational culture definitions and the different performance metrics used to assess organizational cultures. [4]

Through these aspects, organizational culture can be defined as "the specific collection of values and norms shared by people and groups within an organization that influence how they interact with each other and with external stakeholders." [5]

Yet, the most intriguing characteristic of the concept of culture is that it relates to a phenomenon that operates beneath the surface but has a powerful, yet unseen, impact, and to a large extent, most of it happens subconsciously. Culture influences frames of reference and mindsets within individuals in an organization. Marshak described these frames of reference as one of the primary covert processes we perform daily at work. [6]

The previously discussed definition of culture covers organizational values, including DEI and beliefs about the goals members of an organization should pursue. It also addresses the behaviors considered standard or appropriate, and how they should be used to achieve organizational goals.

These organizational values lead to organizational norms, which are the expectations or guidelines that indicate appropriate behavior for employees in various situations. They also aim to regulate how members of the organization interact with one another.

To gain increased insights into a culture, Schein divided it into three levels:

- Artifacts
- Espoused Beliefs and Values
- Basic Underlying Assumptions

Schein (Figure 1) pointed out that the 'basic underlying assumptions' are the most important of the bunch in the following words:

"Human minds need cognitive stability, and any challenge to a basic assumption will release anxiety and defensiveness."

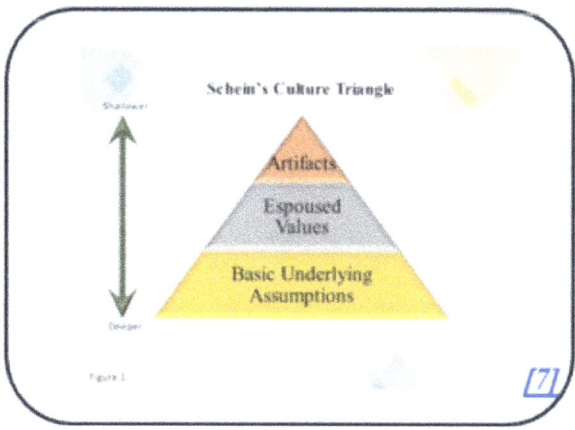

Corporate culture: Is it the same as organizational culture?

Many people confuse organizational culture with corporate culture, but they are very different. Organizational culture has a wider scope with more complex ideas, focusing on what an organization 'is' rather than what it 'has.'

On the other hand, corporate culture includes the customs, values, meanings, and traditions that distinguish a company. It is often referred to as the 'character of an organization' because it clearly reflects the vision of the organization's founders. Corporate culture values also shape the company's managerial behavior and ethical standards.

Senior management plays a crucial role in shaping the corporate culture. They may want to establish standards and values that align with specific organizational goals. Additionally, the workforce already contains internal cultures. Different work groups within the organization have unique behaviors and quirks that influence the entire system to some extent.

The four-culture typology by Roger Harrison [8] suggests that corporate culture, unlike organizational culture, can be 'imported.' For example, a lab technician will carry language, expertise, and behavior independently of the organization. However, their presence will influence the entire organizational culture. It is often said that you can take the individual out of Philadelphia and relocate them to Dallas, and they will still prefer a Philly steak over a hot dog.

John McCann says, "Culture is the way we do things around here. Too often, individuals have heard this phrase within six months of their new assignment. The culture, better known as the unwritten rules, lets individuals know where they stand as someone new in a workgroup."

Culture vs. Climate

The climate is often confused with culture. Although they are not the same, they are linked. The climate shows how things are. It reflects how most people feel about a typical day. Culture is the personality of the organization. It is the shared set of beliefs of the group. Culture allows the climate to behave as it does (Gruenert & Whitaker, 2017, pp. 3–4) when something happens. Once an event impacts the climate repeatedly, it becomes part of the culture.

What defines culture?

If an individual were to search for a short definition of culture, then it would entail the following elements:

1. Values: Their behavioral standards. What is important in their life?
2. Beliefs: the way they think their creed and ideology
3. Traditions are their belief patterns and practices that were handed down to them by people before them.
4. Customs: A widely accepted way of doing something from where they come.
5. Habits: Their typical behavioral manners and patterns
6. Biases: their inclination toward or against someone or something
7. Prejudices: Their prejudgment of specific groups

The question does arise, however, regarding the origin of these beliefs, customs, values, habits, and traditions. According to Morris Massey, the sources of all these factors are usually family, places of worship, friends, peers, educational institutions, and geographical influences. He also explains that these sources and the process of developing specific character traits in an individual or society are called enculturation or socialization.

According to that definition, our culture isn't innate; instead, it's learned behavior influenced by one's environment. Usually, it's passed down through generations; sometimes, it's taught directly.

It bears a symbol, an identity, for someone, much like their unique fingerprint. Once again, the arbitrariness of culture is highlighted; it is intangible, yet it remains what keeps societies functioning. John Norris considers culture a bag, while Peggy McIntosh describes it as a knapsack, and [9] Marilyn Loden and Judy Rosener [10] refer to it as a wheel or lens in their Diversity Wheel model. [11] Whatever the analogy or metaphor, it shows us that no two individuals carry identical cultures, and no two have had the same experiences.

However, a deeper understanding raises the question of similarities within those differences. These similarities define the characteristics of any culture. Shared symbols, common language, collective rituals, and universal values like respect, fairness, and belonging often serve as cultural anchors. These core elements create a sense of unity among diverse groups and connect individual identity with collective experience. Recognizing this balance between uniqueness and shared humanity is essential when navigating multicultural environments, especially in workplaces working toward genuine inclusion and belonging.

Values and Their Development

Values shape how societies, organizations, and individuals behave, what they consider important, and how they work toward their goals. Values are culturally accepted desires that motivate a person's actions. They represent the moral principles of a society, organization, or individual and form the basis for their attitudes, beliefs, and decisions. [12]

No one is born with values; they are formed later in life. According to well-known sociologist Morris Massey [13], values develop during three key periods of a person's life.

The Imprint Period

Children up to age seven are like sponges in their ability to learn; they absorb everything around them and often accept most of the information they receive as truth. Because they lack experience and have underdeveloped judgment, kids are vulnerable to adopting the beliefs of others, especially when those beliefs are taught by people they trust the most, such as their parents. [14]

Often, unintentional impressions can leave a lasting impact on a child's life. Blind trust in parents and confusion during this stage can also lead to issues like early trauma. Additionally, the impression that belief creates can profoundly influence an individual's self-esteem and perceptions.

The modeling period

From age eight until they turn thirteen, children often imitate many people, especially those they see as role models, such as parents, movie stars, musicians, and others. During this stage, they mainly engage in role-playing with their idols in their lives, and most of it is healthy and beneficial for their development.

An individual can develop new beliefs and values by experimenting during the modeling period. It's like trying on different suits to see which one fits best. However, similar to the imprint period, the brain's judgment center is still maturing during this time, resulting in a very low ability to rationally evaluate beliefs. Consequently, most of the values and beliefs encountered are judged based on likes, dislikes, and similar preferences.

The Socialization Period

Between the ages of thirteen and twenty-one, individuals are mostly influenced by their peers. During this developmental stage, the mind becomes more aware, and individuals begin questioning their long-held beliefs, behaviors, and values. Furthermore, the human brain becomes more skeptical during this period and starts forming personal DEIs about morality. They naturally gravitate toward people with similar values as they develop their unique perception of the world. Additionally, in today's age, social media plays a major role in shaping individuals' acceptance of their peers' values.

While the three periods above define the growth of values, they are mostly disorganized, and individuals rarely influence the factors that create those values within them. However, there is a process of becoming more principled in life and developing high moral values that reflect a person's true self rather than those imposed by society. The path to building high morals involves three stages: [15]

Pre-Moral

At this stage, an individual does not possess any actual values, making them what can be called an 'amoral' being. Adolescents are pre-moral, but so are psychopaths. Basic human nature highlights Machiavellian behavior: to use any means necessary to achieve goals, even if it involves hurting others.

Conventional

Most people hold a traditional set of values, often learned from their teachers, parents, and peers. These values mean saying, 'These rules are here for you to live at peace with others.' The core of these values is flexibility: people follow those they are supposed to for as long as they need them.

They will occasionally break those values, especially when there is a threat to their needs and they are confident they can get away with it without notice.

Principled

When individuals are principled, they believe in their values deeply and at the core of their being. These values reside within them subconsciously and are a vital part of who they are. To these individuals, the concepts of right and wrong are absolute and go beyond their personal identity. Like their beliefs, they are defined by a purpose or religion.

Principled individuals stick to their values, whatever the circumstances, and would rather sacrifice themselves than break their values. Most of the great leaders who came into the world were principled.

Why do values matter?

Cultural differences, such as age and nationality, are less significant than the various perspectives and values that arise from these differences. An individual's cultural values strongly influence how they communicate, interact, execute tasks, and plan. Some common cultural values shared worldwide include:

- Individualism and collectivism: These cultural values emphasize personal rights and individual goals versus group relationships and goals.
- Low Power Distance/High Power Distance: There is a stress on shared decision-making and equality as compared to status differences and the absence of autonomy in decisions.
- Cooperative or competitive: provides an emphasis on family, nurturing, and a collaborative environment as opposed to an achievement-based, assertive, and competitive environment.
- Short-term or long-term. Simply put, these values emphasize short-term outcomes rather than long-term planning.
- Being/Doing – Focuses on quality of life versus goal orientation and a busy schedule.
- Monochronic, linear, or polychronic, non-linear. Gives preference to working on a single thing at a time and punctuality as opposed to interruptions and multitasking.

When it comes to understanding basic cultural differences worldwide, cultural value dimensions play a crucial role. Understanding the dynamics of team dynamics and your role within it can provide valuable insights into fostering a more inclusive workplace culture.

Cultural Beliefs

Cultural beliefs are the beliefs that are shared and learned among different groups of people. Since the amount of information in any culture is too large for any one person to master completely, individuals follow different subsets of cultural knowledge, which leads to differences in cultures. [16]

Belief systems are normative frameworks that are interconnected and mainly differ systematically. They form the foundation of any moral code, philosophy, or religion. However, what is systematic in belief systems is the way different beliefs are related to each other. Belief systems are stories people tell themselves to give their sense of reality some kind of meaning. [17]

Humans tend to rely on all the belief systems available to them to cope with different events in their lives. The natural need to find a sense of purpose makes individuals more likely to follow a set of beliefs. Some common traits of any belief system include the following:

- Personal commitment is one of the most interesting and observable features of any ideology. If personal commitment were out of the window, then the belief system would not reverberate socially with as strong consequences as it currently does.
- Existence: Every belief system carries an existence that is independent of its committed believers. No believer has knowledge of the entire belief system. It is highly unlikely for them to have the know-how over more than a small part of the big equation. Therefore, whether consciously or subconsciously, they must take the rest of the belief system purely on faith.
- Lifespan: The lifespan of the belief is much longer than the lifespan of its believer.
- Boundaries: Most of the time, boundaries in a belief system are undefined, as a collection of beliefs rarely carries clean boundaries. [18]

While there are shared characteristics of any belief system, a belief system must have these elements to be deemed one:

- Values: Whether explicit or implicit, a belief system defines moral parameters such as the notion of value or goodness. This is formulated after that fact; the ideal values become abstract summaries of various behavioral attributes that are rewarded by the social system. Social groups perceive themselves as setting order to multiple things to implement their values justly.
- Language: It forms the logic behind any belief system. There are coherent and logical rules that any belief system carries, which are communicated via language from one belief system to another.
- Perspective: The perspective provides a conceptual tool set for any belief system. Perspective explains the reason behind the presence of certain aspects, and their genesis is the identification and meaning behind any belief system.

There are social implications for how culture influences rituals and traditions, doctrines and institutions, mythology, and beliefs. Culture functions as both a means of subordination and power. Society's values, DEI, and beliefs not only reflect its dominant culture but also help reproduce it.

The attitudes and beliefs shaped by culture are not solely determined by education, words, class, religious beliefs, expressions, symbols, or mass media. Instead, culture is influenced by the harmony among all these elements.

Culture is complex. It is unseen, normal, and we are constantly immersed in it. The more we understand social and organizational culture, the better we can influence the organization toward positive results. David Livermore and the Cultural Intelligence Center introduced the concept of being culturally intelligent into the workplace about 20 years ago. Let's explore how cultural intelligence (CQ) can help us become better leaders.

Cultural Intelligence (CQ)

Cultural intelligence, or CQ, as we call it, relates to national and ethnic differences as well as variations across regional cultures, professional environments, generations, functions, and much more. Leading organizations worldwide, such as Harvard University, the London School of Economics, Coca-Cola, and BMW, utilize CQ. Cultural intelligence (CQ) is the ability to relate to and work effectively in culturally diverse settings, whether local or global. It encompasses cultural sensitivity and awareness but also extends to the skills required for better collaboration with people from diverse backgrounds and plays a vital role in managing bias.

At the core of DEIA is understanding and managing both unconscious and conscious bias. We need to see why managing bias is important and build confidence in discussing it. With high CQ, you're less likely to act on biases. You can control how bias is applied and choose not to act in biased ways intentionally. As we develop our CQ, we learn to shift from reacting unconsciously to making more conscious, deliberate choices. Just like learning any new skill, this may take more time initially. But with practice and over time, it becomes easier and more natural.

Based on research conducted worldwide, four capabilities consistently emerge among people who are considered culturally intelligent.

CQ Drive

CQ Drive reflects your level of interest, persistence, and confidence during multicultural interactions. It serves as the foundation for addressing unconscious bias by measuring your motivation to consider how bias affects yourself and others. Additionally, it helps you understand how persistent and confident you are when confronting bias.

CQ knowledge is your understanding of how cultures are similar and different. Understanding how various aspects of our cultural identities influence the way we think, interact, and work with one another helps us recognize our own biases and those of others.

Cultural Intelligence Mod El (Figure 2)

Cultural Intelligence Model

CQ Drive
Your level of interest, persistence, and Confidence during Multicultural interactions.

CQ Knowledge
Your understanding about how cultures are similar and different.

CQ Action
Your ability to adapt when relating and working in multicultural contexts.

CQ Strategy
Your awareness and ability to plan for multicultural interacts.

Your CQ strategy is your awareness and ability to plan for multicultural interactions. It involves specific strategies used to manage unconscious bias.

CQ action is your ability to adapt when working and interacting in multicultural settings. It's what we discuss today, and we're actually using it to eliminate bias in our relationships and work while promoting diversity, thus fostering a culture of inclusion.

Let's spend some time digging deeper into each of the four CQ capabilities.

It is your level of interest, persistence, and confidence during multicultural interactions.

The culturally intelligent individuals can motivate themselves to put in the extra effort often needed when interacting with and working alongside people from different cultural backgrounds. Imagine your boss telling you that you need to join a task force for the next six weeks, and everyone on the team is from culture X. What culture would make you feel anxious about this assignment? Why?

We all have different cultures that challenge us. It might be due to implicit bias, past experiences, or no experience with the culture beyond what others have told us. Part of engaging CQ Drive is honestly examining the cultures that challenge us rather than pretending we're 'color blind' or claiming we see everyone equally. We don't.

There are many ways you can apply for CQ Drive, including:

Clarify the goal.

Clarity about the goal you're trying to reach is a key way to use your CQ Drive. During times of stress and frustration, we can lose track of the goal. Look at the intercultural situation above. What is the main goal of the task force? Think about how understanding that goal can help you and others push through the challenges of this culture-X situation.

Manage your emotional and physical stamina

Our physical and emotional states, along with our emotional intelligence, directly influence our motivation to understand different cultural perspectives. When we're sick, jet-lagged, or emotionally burdened, it's much harder to put in the effort needed to work with others from diverse backgrounds. Think about how this might affect your CQ drive.

CQ Knowledge

It is your understanding of how cultures are similar and different.

Your CQ knowledge is one of the best ways to better understand intercultural situations that might otherwise leave you confused. CQ

Knowledge provides insights into why people think and act the way they do. It helps you identify when a behavior reflects someone's culture and when it's more likely a reflection of their personality or circumstances.

In the CQ Drive section, you identified the culture or cultures you need to understand most. CQ Knowledge will guide you to find the most relevant information about that culture. For example, one of the cultural value differences we discussed earlier was between direct and indirect communication. Western cultures tend to be more direct, but even within Western cultures, there are differences in how direct they are.

When the British say, "With all due respect," how does it sound to others who interpret it literally? What do the British actually mean? When Southerners say, "Bless your heart," what do they imply? You understand the idea. The more you learn about your CQ, the more you'll be able to use it in intercultural situations you face. Here are a few ways to apply your CQ knowledge:

Determine what part of a situation is cultural.

Remember your cultural challenge? What aspect of this situation is cultural, and what is more related to other variables that are not directly cultural (e.g., organizational issues, stress, personal issues, personalities, etc.)?

Use cultural values to analyze multicultural situations.

The ten cultural values are a powerful way to gain insight into what is happening in an intercultural situation. Start looking for how these situations emerge in your day-to-day conversations.

CQ Strategy

It is your awareness and ability to plan for multicultural interactions that people with high CQ strategy traits refine their mental models and develop high-quality strategies for multicultural interactions.

During this section, we'll explore the importance of anticipating how people from different cultural backgrounds may respond to your actions. Which upcoming multicultural engagement or project could benefit from some extra planning on your part? It might be an upcoming meeting, a presentation to a group from a different culture, or a marketing campaign targeting a different background. CQ Strategy will help you develop strategies without stereotyping. Ask yourself, How does the cultural background of an audience influence the way you prepare a presentation?

CQ strategy involves taking the time to anticipate what kind of presentation style and content will work best for an individual or group based on their cultural background. We often tend to jump to negative conclusions when observing unfamiliar behaviors from people who are different from us. Some questions to ask during an uncomfortable interaction include:

- How is my plan working?
- Is this individual behaving the way he or she typically would, or is he or she adapting to me?

A good way to develop your awareness is to jot down a few observations immediately following an intercultural interaction, including:

- Things that were different from what you anticipated
- Things that are different from how you would do something in your own culture.
- Questions you need to explore further

CQ Action

The final of the four CQ capabilities is CQ action, which is your ability to adapt when interacting with and operating in multicultural settings.

People with high CQ action rely on a wide range of behaviors. The best way to improve our CQ action is through practice. What is one behavior you need to better adapt when interacting with others?

Consider an action or behavior you do that might be interpreted differently by another culture—such as how quickly you speak, how warmly you greet people, or any number of other things.

CQ Action is all about adapting our behavior when a situation calls for it, and it will help you become more comfortable using different methods for work and communication.

There are many ways to practice CQ Action in your life. Essentially, any time you interact with someone from a different cultural background, you are utilizing CQ action. A few ways to do this include the following:

Reduce or clarify Jargon and insider language

Don't assume people know the idioms, acronyms, or terms you use. Be cautious. You don't want to offend by over-explaining or assuming they don't understand, but it's best to use clear, simple language until the other person shows they're familiar with your usual terms.

Mirror your counterpart's communication style

If someone emails you using a formal title, respond in kind. If someone greets you a certain way, try to mirror their greeting (e.g., handshake, hug, bow, etc.). This should be based on your CQ knowledge and strategy to avoid overdoing it or over-adapting. However, in most cases, mirroring your conversation partner's communication style works well, at least initially.

So, with a solid understanding of what culture is and how it functions, along with increasing your CQ drive, knowledge, strategy, and action, you'll immediately notice a difference in how you communicate with your team and how the team interacts with others.

Organizational And Social Cultures Are Transmitted From Generation To Generation.

- Culture is symbolic; it is the language we speak and the food we eat. The elders of the culture are the keepers of the culture. Respect, intelligence, professionalism, and timeliness are cultural.
- We all have varying amounts of cultural intelligence. The more we utilize the model as a planning tool, the more our CQ drive, knowledge, strategy, and action will increase.
- Positive cultures value mistakes. Toxic cultures attempt to obstruct change and hide mistakes. This is often accomplished in a completely subconscious way.
- In the next chapter, we'll look at the talents of members of your team who are the backbone of your success—the team player. Their contributions are frequently immeasurable. They are not impossible to find, but much easier to develop.

Chapter 9
VUCA - The Nature of Our World

It always seems IMPOSSIBLE until it's done.
--- Nelson Mandela

On April 3, the United States began implementing new tariffs worldwide. These initial tariffs ranged from 10% to over 50% on products imported into the country. That move triggered other nations to retaliate with their own tariffs on the U.S. As a result, within 48 hours, MSNBC reported a historic warning: the stock market had lost more than $6.4 trillion. How did we arrive here? Did we see this coming? More importantly, where do we go from here? It's clear there was a global sense of concern and disbelief about the situation. This book cannot answer these key questions, but it can offer some insight into the dynamic environment in which this occurred.

VUCA and Its Nature

It's time to start discussing some of the larger acronyms and words that are rarely used in managerial or leadership contexts. Do you know what VUCA is? Although most people may not be familiar with the definition or meaning of VUCA, many of us have had the opportunity to experience this phenomenon. When it occurs, most will understand its significance. The general business press and academic literature have employed various terms over the past few decades to describe our growing inability to comprehend the world and navigate the traumatic events around us. Some lingering examples include flux, dynamism, disruption, complexity, hyper-competition, Fog of war, continuous white water, fast-moving marketplaces, and turbulence. VUCA, an acronym for Volatility, Uncertainty, Complexity, and Ambiguity, captures the essence of today's global economic and political landscape. Leaders across industries are increasingly challenged to adapt in real-time, make decisions with incomplete information, and maintain stability in environments that are anything but stable. Understanding VUCA isn't just an academic exercise; it's a necessary lens through which to view modern-day leadership, strategy, and survival.

Fundamentals of VUCA

These terms are used to describe the characteristics of the environment we find ourselves in. Each term clearly outlines the unique circumstances the user observes. These multiple terms are condensed into "VUCA," which has become popular in recent years to describe the many aspects of this "uncontrollable" environment. Recently, this term has been used to characterize the changing world. But what does it mean to live, function, and lead in a VUCA world?

VUCA is definitely an acronym. It stands for Volatile, Uncertain, Complex, and Ambiguous. Several explanations are available, including a Wikipedia page and an essay by Nathan Bennett and G. James Lemoine in the Harvard Business Review. Nonetheless, some additional explanations might be helpful to support these reasons.

In this chapter, I plan to explore the concept of VUCA further, examine if the world is growing more VUCA, and discuss what this means for business. Let me start by briefly outlining the four components.

Volatility, uncertainty, complexity, and ambiguity, or VUCA, make situations or conditions difficult to predict, assess, respond to, or plan for. Understanding how to mitigate these traits can greatly improve a leader's strategic skills and lead to better outcomes.

The trait of being volatile involves being prone to frequent, rapid, and significant change. Small events can cause major shifts. For example, in a turbulent market, commodity prices might spike or fall sharply in a short time, and a trend's direction can suddenly shift.

When events and results are unpredictable, uncertainty ensues. The link between causes and effects becomes unclear. Therefore, prior knowledge might not be applicable in such cases. The future is uncertain; for example, in a volatile market, it is hard to predict if and how much prices will rise or fall.

Complexity involves many interconnected problems. It's hard to understand how things and people relate to each other. A change in one area can unintentionally cause changes in other areas. Many layers obscure cause and effect, making it unclear which elements are key to the decision-making process. For example, in a complex market, gas price changes can affect the costs of unrelated goods.

Lack of clarity and difficulties understanding the specifics of the situation create ambiguity. This can lead to mistakes or misinterpretations. When circumstances are unclear, all the facts become murky. Participants might not be aware of the objective or desired outcome. For example, in an unclear market, not all information is available, and hidden forces can affect pricing.

VUCA was first used in 1987 at the American Army War College, and Herbert Barber popularized it in 1991 (2). The concept was developed from ideas in Warren Bennis and Burt Nanus's book Leaders (3): The Techniques for Taking Control. Conditions after the Cold War's end and the war in Afghanistan were described as VUCA.

VUCA is a term that can describe various situations. It is sometimes used dismissively to downplay the importance of planning. The harmful remark, "Due to the current VUCA, any plans we make will quickly become obsolete and meaningless, so why bother planning?" can be made. In this way, its use is comparable to FUD (fear, uncertainty, and doubt).

VUCA should be used to assess a situation to help estimate risks and develop mitigation strategies. When analyzing a situation or strategy, apply the VUCA framework to determine what is known and what is unknown. This enhances understanding of the situation, including its weaknesses and threats. VUCA can support leaders in navigating the ever-changing nature of today's corporate environment.

The four terms are connected in real life. For example, the more complex and chaotic an industry is, the harder it is to predict, and as a result, the more unpredictable it becomes. However, each of the four represents a different factor that makes our environment—the planet, a market, or an industry—difficult to understand and manage.

There is a lot of quick but predictable change in a world that is only volatile (and not uncertain, complex, or ambiguous). Conversely, in a completely unpredictable environment, it is difficult to foresee how events will unfold (but not volatile, complex, or ambiguous). Additionally, things are hard to clarify and understand in a purely complicated (but not volatile, uncertain, or ambiguous) world. Lastly, things are simply hard to grasp in a strictly vague (but not volatile, uncertain, or complex) world.

A VUCA situation

In a thought exercise, the following questions can be used to determine the VUCA in a situation:

Volatility. What are the highest and lowest possible values? How quickly can these values change? How much fluctuation can we tolerate before it harms us?

Uncertainty. What is subject to change? What potential signs of change are there? Will we receive alerts if anything shifts? How fast can we adjust to change?

Complexity. How well do we understand the underlying structures? How are these things connected? What is the extent of our ability to stop a domino effect or cascading failure?

Ambiguity. How clearly do we understand internal and external factors? What are the chances of confusion and misunderstanding?

How can instructions be given more precisely? What indicates that more data is needed before making a decision?

VUCA can help people

VUCA helps people recognize potential surprises and outcomes. They can then create plans to mitigate and respond to sudden changes in VUCA environments. They become better prepared to move from "unknown unknowns" to "known unknowns." Leaders can also utilize the observing, orienting, deciding, and acting (OODA) loop for effective decision-making.

- Volatility. Recognize change. Allow flexibility and margin for unexpected issues.
- Uncertainty. Make the effort to understand triggers and signs, and seek new perspectives. Monitor important metrics and include markers for success and failure at each stage. Keep port modems and conduct regular reviews. Use hypothetical scenarios to train personnel and prepare for unexpected events.
- Complexity. Keep communication open with all parties. Encourage cooperation among groups and teams. Identify areas needing further insight and add talent to address them, including backup and fail-safe systems.
- Ambiguity. Run tests to clarify unclear information. Be ready to adapt as new knowledge is gained.

Experts may have differing views in the constantly changing world of technology. Transnational supply chains and related systems are complex and hard to understand. New disruptive technologies are introduced every day. Therefore, the technical framework can greatly benefit from applying the VUCA principles.

VUCA and I & I

The financial crisis, new business analytics, artificial intelligence, constantly evolving corporate models, and the unique COVID-19 virus outbreak established a new standard for work-from-home policies, social isolation, and other factors, but they are not the only reasons the world has changed. However, future needs such as analytical thinking, creative thinking, resilience, flexibility, and agility are even more critical. Where will the resources come from to address these shortages in the next five years?

These changes can occasionally be gradual but rarely as abrupt as the recent COVID-19 crisis the millennial generation experienced. Thus, a VUCA paradigm represents an unstable environment with multiple variables and the potential for relentless change.

The most important factors to consider when discussing workforce I & I are gender and age diversity. A related study by Rajesh, Ekambaram, Rakesh, & Kumar (4) showed that managing gender diversity in the workforce is the key aspect of workforce diversity in a VUCA environment. Organizations have worked hard over the past ten years to be more inclusive of women and the LGBT community. Examples of these efforts include talent management, which involves attracting, hiring, developing, and retaining talent while also acknowledging the differences between men's and women's aspirations and preferred working styles.

We believe that the main factor affecting corporate performance is leadership. In a VUCA world, great leaders understand that change is not discretely scheduled; it may ebb but never completely vanish. These executives foster agility, adaptation, and inclusiveness within their firms, giving them a competitive edge. As they navigate uncertain situations, they anticipate surprises and know which people, processes, or technological levers to pull.

Companies are emphasizing inclusion and diversity more than ever. Millennials and Generation Y are demanding it. Women's Leadership programs and workshops on the intergenerational workforce are highly sought after by HR professionals. Courses on unconscious bias are extremely popular in Silicon Valley. The commitment is genuine, and raising awareness is an important first step.

Nonetheless, some programs aim to "repair" individuals rather than systems. Workshops on unconscious bias can backfire by increasing exclusion and failing to change behavior. Efforts to comply with Title VII may check the box but don't lead to real change; beyond paperwork, workplaces remain just as universe and unwelcoming as before.

So, what works? First and foremost, senior leadership states that an inclusive culture is desired and essential for the company's growth. There is a diversity dividend. Next, a multifaceted strategy

1. Provide a solid and convincing business case for inclusion. Every leader needs to be aware of how important inclusion is to their ability to produce success.
2. Encourage collaboration and an agile mindset among leaders by providing them with practice using the appropriate routines, attitudes, and language. Encourage this mentality at work.
3. Train individuals to audit their procedures and systems and improve their equity.
4. Use strategies that have been proven to help modify beliefs and actions. Social scientists have demonstrated ways to alter basic beliefs, enabling individuals to alter their behavior and judgment.

Many believe the corporate environment will keep becoming more volatile, unclear, complex, and ambiguous. If you want to manage teams in the VUCA era, you need to be aware of the changes this environment might bring.

A VUCA situation can

- Cause people to become uneasy and destabilized.
- Take away their drive.
- Obstruct their attempts to advance their careers.
- Make it mandatory to retrain and reshape constantly.
- Fighting requires a lot of time and energy.

- Raise the likelihood that people will make poor decisions.
- Stifle the ability to make decisions.
- Endanger long-term initiatives, advancements, and breakthroughs.
- Overpower people and organizations.
- Have an impact on the corporate culture.
- "Bleed" within enterprises to generate VUCA conditions.

If this environment impacts your industry or organization, you need to reevaluate how you and your company operate.

The narrative in Figure 1, "Navigating the World of Tariffs," illustrates how a shift in government policies can have widespread effects, regardless of intent.

Businesses now must contend with sophisticated services and products, unexpected changes, and constantly shifting market conditions that influence consumer decisions in a world where technological advancements, rapid digitization, and national barriers have disappeared.

The most important factors in preventing and resolving past crises and issues were reducing ambiguity, having strong analytical skills, and acting quickly. However, given today's circumstances, ambiguity is unavoidable.

Traditional management methods are outdated. Effective strategic management requires seamless process management, and without integrating these methods and tools smoothly into the system, they will be ineffective. Proper risk management is also crucial. Only a VUCA-based, precise management strategy can influence these techniques, tools, and systems. Implementing this management approach may make these strategies, instruments, and platforms ineffective and lead to additional business expenses.

A review of the relevant national and international literature shows that the VUCA issue has been addressed by a very small number of research studies. Most experts, professionals, and practitioners agree that VUCA is a persistent phenomenon whose impact will only increase over time.

The VUCA phenomenon shapes the modern environment, where traditional leadership skills are no longer enough, and reformulating decisions occurs at the leadership level. Leaders' ability to navigate uncertainty is vital in the VUCA era. Today's corporate landscape is characterized by volatility, uncertainty, complexity, and ambiguity.

The term "VUCA" is an abbreviation derived from a military phrase used by the US Army to describe the unpredictability, controversies, and doubts surrounding the multipolar world order that arose after the USSR and the US declared the end of the Cold War era (5). To develop a distinct mindset, clear vision, and greater flexibility in strategic activities like attack, defense, and combat training, the concept of VUCA was established (6).

The concept of VUCA has been used to reduce the suffering that institutions and individuals experience when dealing with complex phenomena that are unknown and unseen, from its origin to the present day. It has been applied across a wide range, from state politics to everyday decisions made by people (7).

VUCA describes the complex and ever-changing business environment that companies and individuals must navigate. Although the term VUCA, often used in political contexts, has become closely associated with the economic world in modern times. Uncertainty has shifted from something that businesses could plan to eliminate to a reality that companies must learn to operate within. However, to manage this effectively and successfully, managers and leaders must adopt a flexible and proactive approach (8). Reactive behavior is the last thing managers and leaders should engage in. Instead, they need to focus on building the future first.

The VUCA phenomena highlight today's corporate environment's inevitable complexity, ambiguity, uncertainty, and volatility. Most people seek different ways to manage and plan under strong leadership. Failing to address the challenges caused by VUCA will cause firms to fall behind in this fast-paced, highly dynamic era. We are experiencing VUCA phenomena due to events like Brexit, the coronavirus (Covid-19), refugee and immigration issues, environmental shifts, and more.

Due to the global impact of the VUCA phenomenon, it is currently very difficult to generate profitability and growth by gaining a lasting competitive advantage. The organization, its executives, and its workers must recognize VUCA, use appropriate management models, and develop sensible strategies. VUCA, which is considered a component of organizations, influences their stakeholders' internal and external environments and affects all parameters and variables, including risk management, crisis management, internal entrepreneurship, leadership, communication, and decision-making processes.

The leadership and management paradigms previously used are no longer relevant because the business environments in which companies operate are becoming increasingly complex every day. Leading and managing in today's global and corporate landscape requires handling complex data. Therefore, new leadership and management approaches must be adopted. Addressing the challenges of the VUCA world and market issues, it is essential to encourage and support employees in offering fresh perspectives, generating innovative ideas, being creative, gaining flexibility, challenging norms, and developing responsible leadership styles that are generous, capable of fostering business ideas and networking, and attentive to ethical principles.

In today's VUCA environment, managers and leaders need to recognize opportunities within challenges. Developing networks for organization, management, and decision-making

is vital to balance opportunities and risks. As complexity surpasses our ability to adapt, and business practices and technology continue to evolve, decision-making must occur amid ambiguity in a highly volatile market and industry landscape.

Collaboration by Leaders and Managers

In the VUCA (Volatility, Uncertainty, Complexity, Ambiguity) business environment, effective leadership and management must work closely together to navigate challenges and achieve organizational success. Leadership offers the vision and motivation, while management handles execution and operational efficiency. Together, they develop a unified strategy that enables organizations to adapt and prosper.

Benefits of Discussing VUCA Elements

1. Anticipate and Respond to Volatility: Develop strategies to manage rapid and unpredictable changes.
2. Make Decisions Amid Uncertainty: Enhance decision-making skills in the face of limited information.
3. Manage Complexity: Understand and address intricate interdependencies within systems.
4. Embrace Ambiguity: Foster a culture of innovation and adaptability.
    a. Accomplishments After Reading the Book
    b. Upon concluding this book, leaders and managers will be able to:
        - Enhance Strategic Vision: Develop a clear and adaptable vision for the organization.
        - Improve Decision-Making: Make informed and timely decisions that drive success.

- Boost Employee Engagement: Foster a positive work environment that enhances productivity.
- Build Organizational Resilience: Create a resilient organization capable of thriving in dynamic conditions.
   - Incorporating Insights into the Work Environment
   - To incorporate the insights from this book into their work environment, leaders and managers should:
- Promote Continuous Learning: Encourage ongoing development and adaptation to new challenges.
- Foster Collaboration: Ensure that leadership and management work together seamlessly.
- Implement Agile Practices: Adopt flexible and responsive strategies to navigate VUCA challenges.
- Cultivate Innovation: Create an environment that encourages creativity and new ideas.

By understanding and addressing the challenges of VUCA, leaders and managers can develop the skills necessary to navigate the complexities of the modern business world. This book will provide you with the tools and insights needed to enhance your leadership and management capabilities, preparing you to lead effectively in a dynamic and ever-changing environment.

Implications for Leadership And Management

A thorough understanding of this concept and its implications for leadership and management in today's dynamic business environment is crucial. It emphasizes the need for leaders to adapt to these challenges and develop strategies to navigate the complexities of modern markets. It's all about how these factors make the business world super unpredictable and challenging. Leaders need to be flexible and ready to handle these crazy changes, and a good understanding of these final points will do just that:

- Definition of VUCA: VUCA, or Volatility, Uncertainty, Complexity, and Ambiguity, will always embody the challenges leaders face in evaluating and responding to dynamic environments. VUCA is a fancy way of saying things that can change fast, outcomes are hard to predict, problems are interconnected, and situations can be unclear.

- Characteristics of VUCA: Volatility refers to rapid and significant changes, uncertainty highlights unpredictable outcomes, complexity involves interrelated problems, and ambiguity points to unclear situations.
- Historical Context: The term VUCA originated in military contexts in the late 1980s, particularly after the Cold War, and has since been adapted to describe business environments.
- Impact of VUCA on Business: Companies must recognize VUCA as a persistent phenomenon affecting risk management, decision-making, and organizational strategies.
- Leadership in a VUCA World: Effective leaders foster agility and inclusivity, preparing their organizations for unexpected changes while leveraging diverse perspectives and skills.
- Diversity and Inclusion: Emphasizing gender and age diversity is crucial as organizations strive to create inclusive environments that enhance performance in a VUCA (volatile, uncertain, complex, and ambiguous) landscape.
- Strategic Approaches: Leaders should implement proactive management models that embrace VUCA principles, focusing on collaboration, communication, and flexibility to navigate complexities.
- Future Considerations: Understanding VUCA is essential for organizations to thrive amid ongoing changes and challenges in the global business landscape.

Chapter 10
Leadership and Management Strategies

"Success comes from having the proper aim as well as the right ammunition."
                                                Quality Air Force

Let's try this. When I started working at a new location and company, I was always excited to get the lay of the land. Usually, I drove to the sites to ensure I could find a parking spot. Seriously, this lowered my anxiety on day one. I knew the route to the office and how much time I would need. Or, as was the case when I had to catch a bus, knowing the corner where the bus would stop was crucial.

Looking back on these events might seem a bit silly now, but they didn't at the time. They helped reduce my nervousness, and these actions made the first day at work more comfortable. The main point is to do whatever it takes to be prepared to make a strong impression on day one. If we want to feel confident in our organization, doing recon is always a good idea. As the leader, you need to assess the status of your unit. The sooner, the better. How do you do that? I believe the following approach will help you get there.

Generally, you have a few methods to gain the knowledge you will need to perform your job:

- Ask your new boss. However, they might not be fully aware of all the changes in your section, since they are insiders. I have found that even the SOPs are not always fully followed by workers.
- Ask the person who held the post before you (they, too, may have forgotten the most critical aspects of the job).
- Learn as you go (OJT). This is the most popular.
- Let your experience lead the way. Be careful that

old experiences are just that --- old but not forgotten.

*None of these is foolproof for a lot of reasons.

We want to avoid making mistakes when starting a new job, or we might not last long there; if they keep us, we might not be enough for a good while. I believe there are more reliable methods. I have always aimed to use a systematic approach, which has worked well, but I recently found that adding an executive coach can help with the adaptation process.

These options create a strong team. I strongly support providing each new employee, especially at the executive level, with an executive coach (possibly a mentor), conducting an organizational assessment, and attending a change management training workshop within 30 days of taking on the role. The following sections aim to introduce a development strategy for new employees. They should provide insights into these highly effective areas and, more importantly, what to consider when leading an "Exclusion to Inclusion" campaign. These elements should improve an already comprehensive orientation program.

Executive Coach

My personal and professional experience has shown me that when you prepare individuals for the events they will face, they tend to adapt more quickly and perform better than those who are not given such information. I will share a real-world experience from my days playing football. The week before we were set to face a conference rival, our coaches were determined to stop them from effectively using one of their favorite plays. We analyzed their film and practiced against our own practice team. We even assigned a call sign to alert us when they attempted it. We were so well prepared that, when they ran it in the actual game, all eleven of us shouted the signal together. And we stopped them cold.

Effective and focused executive coaching does the same. I worked with a high-potential employee around an observation that sometimes new executives unconsciously believe that what got them there is the key to their future success. Malcolm Goldsmith's book (Jan 2007) titled "What Got You Here, Won't Get You There" is a great read to gain more insights into these phenomena. You must examine his list of 20 habits to avoid. In short, the real message is that we must continue to learn and develop.

Therefore, I strongly recommend and endorse leaders and organizations to support an initiative that promotes Executive Coaching. Here is a strawman for a program I have implemented in some organizations.

Be aware that this type of initiative will require funding. Most agencies do not have professional Executive Coaches in their Human Resources Department or even on an individual basis. Therefore, set aside a budget for it. Potential costs will be addressed later.

An Agency Coaching Program Outline

Coaching Philosophy and Guidance

Coaching is a focused, one-on-one professional relationship aimed at speeding up the growth and effectiveness of high potentials within the organization. It is usually linked to key positions where development support is needed. Even if a new executive requests a coach, the organization's leader formally makes the request and approves the support. As a result, the cost of a coaching session typically ranges from $250 to $450 per hour for each coachee.

A strong mentorship program can greatly assist during

this transition. However, be aware that mentoring differs significantly from coaching. A coach offers a cost-effective approach, considering the time it typically takes for a new employee to adjust. Data shows that most new executives need 12-18 months to acclimate to their new role. During this period, the new employee might face issues that could harm their careers and the company's reputation.

Executive coaching can accelerate the organization's onboarding process by reducing it to 6-9 months. Therefore, organizations lacking internal resources like executive coaches should budget for it. On the other hand, not everyone needs coaching, nor does it have to last for several months. Based on my experience, coaching can be highly effective in less than three months.

The overarching goal is to produce observable, measurable, and commensurate results with the performance requirements

of the person being coached, the organization, and most importantly the boss who authorized the resource. Any coaching engagement must be behaviorally or performance-based. This means it aims to increase awareness, accelerate development, and align the coachee with organizational goals.

This means the coach and coachee must work toward:

A specific topic or area of development that has been agreed upon with the supervisor.

- A coaching relationship that focuses on one specific goal or topic at a time. Typically, the length of an engagement ranges from three to six months and addresses two or three of the supervisor's concerns for this new executive.
- In addition, they add or continue workshops (such as

those on diversity and inclusion) that will also enhance their pursuit of leadership. This, too, can cost the agency, but the benefits, in my experience, have consistently yielded a positive return on investment.

At the end of a coaching engagement (6-12 months), the coachee will improve their productivity in relation to the supervisor's goals and objectives. Therefore, coaching is one developmental tool available to employees and should be used alongside the full range of training and development opportunities. The focus of this initiative is to provide strategic coaching engagements to develop leaders, enhance technical excellence, and build effective organizations to achieve mission success.

Who and what roles should you consider for executive coaching support after yourself?

- High-potential and key roles: coaching for supervisors, senior leaders, executives, and high-potential leadership development.
- Accelerated learning and development for change management initiatives, diversity and inclusion initiatives, team-building efforts, and effective leadership
- Transition - Engagements structured around transition best practices, the needs of the individual being coached, and the specific organizational context. Coaching will target executives and supervisors within their first year of appointment.
- Targeted - Engagements are designed to tackle a specific, well-defined issue. A team of coaches will be brought in to provide on-the-job, just-in-time coaching on a particular topic to a large audience

within a short period (i.e., 2-3 days).
- Skill/Topic – Engagements focused on a specific, clearly defined leadership subject (e.g., leadership presence, goal setting, and work unit advocacy). Coaching will cater to the individual's needs.

Sometimes, more time may be required to achieve various goals. Please consider when:

- Funding is available.
- Time is needed to work on the same topic addressed in the original coaching engagement.
- The job changes and requires new skill sets.

Consider that coaching engagements are approved if

- There is funding to support a new engagement.
- Coaching is the appropriate developmental tool for an employee, given their desired outcomes and current situation.
- The request is in line with the Agency coaching philosophy and falls within one of the strategic coaching options/areas.
- Coaching is encouraged by the employee's supervisor.

Consider that coaching engagements are not approved if

- Coaching is used as a remedial action or performance management tool.
- Other development opportunities are considered first, such as a leadership development course/program.
- The employee's supervisor is not supportive of

a coaching engagement.
- The request is not in line with the agency coaching philosophy and does not fall within one of the strategic coaching options/areas.
- There is no funding to support a new engagement.

Communication between Coach and Client

- Phone coaching is the primary method of communication during a coaching engagement. Face-to-face coaching is available if the coach is located near your center. A ZOOM call might be the best solution.
- Clients and coaches are encouraged to utilize technology when their coaching conversation calls for a connection beyond a phone call.

Organization Assessment

We all conduct assessments when we join new organizations or take on a new job. Initially, we assess the individuals around us, then the facilities and equipment, and don't forget the product or service you went there to contribute. Sometimes, these inquiries proceed with, "Why am I here?" This should lead you to a proper assessment process. As the leader, you want to answer all of these questions, and when the first three are answered, you will have the answer to the central question of why I am here.

An Organizational Climate Assessment Outline

Here is what you need to do

My purpose here is to assist you in establishing your climate assessment team. It will give you and your team the basics for an organizational assessment. First, let me be clear, an elementary survey is a part of the assessment, albeit its core. So, this guide will take you from getting the pencils and paper to a review of our assessment. This could be done in as few as five steps to conduct a full-blown assessment. However, for it to be meaningful, complete, and inclusive; I suggest this eight-step approach:

1. The pre-preparation stages
2. Prepare organization members for an upcoming survey
3. Conduct survey
4. Interpret the data
5. Develop briefing for the agency leader
6. Conduct the leadership briefing
7. Extend briefing to the organizational members
8. Conduct hot wash session with the assessment team.

This list may seem long, but this design will include more necessary people in the process than if you were significantly simplified by hiring someone to come in and conduct the survey. I hope you will see my point when you complete this section and run your own assessment.

1. The pre-preparation stages.
    - I believe that to conduct a project, you first need to identify the essential elements required to initiate and complete it. I was once told that when you are exhaustive in your preparation, the battle is half won. For example, if you plan to build a house, yes, you will need wood and bricks, but you also must start with acquiring the land. Don't assume anything. In large organizations, this could be as many as 15-20 people. Communication is the key here. More people will impact this function, so control it here.

- Identify team members and their availability.
- Ensure team diversity (especially ages, work experience, pay grade, indeed the traditional diversity categories, ERG, and thinking).
- Locate a facility for them to meet (private, comfortable, and near the leader).
- Consider the size of the team. Usually, 3–4 core members could be expanded to include additional advisors.
- Train the team on their purpose and focus (to include privacy information), measurement, briefing preparations, equal opportunity advisors, similar employment opportunity specialists/managers, sexual assault response coordinators, victim advocates, legal advisors, inspector generals, and chaplains.
- You must select a survey instrument.
- Obtain subject matter experts to conduct analysis.
- Make sure the survey addresses the concerns you have and potential problems. These can be added to the survey instrument.
- Make sure the survey includes a demographic sheet.
- Determine if it is to be taken on individual sheets of paper or electronically.
- Control the number of questions.

2. Prepare organization members for an upcoming survey

- You now have your team in place; start with identifying the problems as you see them.
- Their tenure on this project should not exceed two weeks.
- They must become familiar with the entire assessment process and their role in it. Therefore, they will require some level of focused training.

- Decide you will make the public presentations and directly interact with the leader.
- Discuss the possible issues with a subject matter expert (SME).

3. Conduct a survey.

- This may seem simple, but it isn't. The team will need to complete several tasks. With input from the leader, the team will choose a survey instrument and determine how it will be distributed to the organization's members. The team will also need to decide whether to conduct the survey online or on paper.
- Members must be advised of the upcoming survey and its purpose. This communication effort will need to be led by the head of the organization. I have seen it done in the briefing, official staff meetings, a written letter from the leader, and weekly flyers. The primary purpose of this communication barrage is to turn out the survey response and not to campaign for a position on the issues.
- We strongly recommend a Likert scale of 1-5 or 1-7. Those who are doing the analysis should be involved in the scale selection. Sometimes, you can use a survey from an external source. This should be a good alternative, especially if they have the database to support their analysis. Make sure their database includes similar organizations with your characteristics. Also, the cost is a consideration. If you have an assessment department, you could quickly develop your own survey instrument.

4. Interpret the data.

- The survey analysis is most critical because it will be the fundamental data and source for making change

creditable. There will be quantitative and qualitative data gathered and produced for the multiple briefing.
- The main reason being is to identify the problem.
- After you have collected all surveys or they were completed online, it is time to gather the data and analyze it.
- This is not easy work. You must analyze and interpret what you have gathered. The purpose of which is to define and understand the root causes of each issue.
- More importantly, to document the end-state of each problem for resolution.
- The SME will be most useful here.
- Define and clarify the problem.
- Contributing factors like people, corporate systems and processes, and physical factors that may contribute to the presenting problem.
- List comprehensive alternatives to these problems.
- Note the emotions and tensions that are associated with these issues.

The following example outlines how to develop two charts to display how to organize and present the survey data from your assessment.

5. Outline for briefings

EXAMPLE Problem: HR Office not processing or tracking personnel actions promptly

Survey Factor Organizational Effectiveness Sub Factor: Organizational Processes

- Process all current Personnel Actions within the next 72hours.
- Process all future Personnel Actions within 48 hours of receipt.

- Use our IT Department to develop a tracking database for temporary Personnel Actions.

Analyze Courses Of Action (COA)
- Next, analyze the COAs and determine how realistic they are at this time. Use measures like time, cost, constraints, impact, and disadvantages as an advantage. Are there gaps, and what are they, if any? Note and document the consequences as a follow-up method.
- The next Course of Action is to select the COA. When choosing, go long term, e.g., six months or even a year. How will it impact the people, the organization? Is it worth it? Does the organization have the resources? Who has the authority to make it happen? Your answers will help the leader to make informed decisions.
- The next step is for the team to develop the action plan using and prioritizing the COA.
    - Prioritize the COA.
    - Note the requirements, be specific.
    - Set a timeline.
    - Identify the resources needed to complete the COA.
6. Conduct the leadership briefings. Now let's develop COA that will lead to change and improvement strategies per personnel concerns. We will use this time to prepare our brief for the boss and the overall management team. This will be a total team effort to identify the real problems and include your team's ideas and opinions. SMEs may also be called in to assess your findings.

Brief the plan to leadership and follow that with a briefing to all personnel. In addition, get feedback for possible modification of the program.

7. Extend briefing to the organization members. Develop and brief the whole plan and results. This must be with the leader's input. So, it must not be shared with anyone until the leader okays its release. My advice is to limit it to a 30-minute session, but you can conduct multiple sessions.

8 Conduct a Hot Wash session with the assessment team. Hot Wash is the opportunity for the team and leadership to see the impact of their work.

- What was our objective?
- Did we hit the target?
- Did we miss it?
- How and where did we miss it?
- Did we have the right team?
- How could we make it better?
- Did we make the points in our briefings?

Other factors to be considered in coaching

- Coachee and organizations will also benefit from assessments, data collection, feedback, etc.
- Modifications of hours require a point of contact for review.
- Who will review possible additional engagements?
- Agency coaching philosophy, guidance, and processes must be followed when using corporate funding.
- When more than one coachee is using a coach, make sure you take advantage of the diversity of thought by using more than one coach per unit.

Change Management

Change Management – An Overview

This section will assist leaders in understanding the field of change management. To do this, I have narrowed it down to three main areas of focus: understanding change management, recognizing the need for change, and efforts to sustain and improve the change initiatives that have been put into place. So far, we have discussed coaching and conducting organizational assessments. The insights from these sections will be very helpful in implementing any change initiatives you may want to pursue.

We know that change is the only constant in our lives. When we lead organizations, our challenge becomes managing that change. Therefore, there are several questions to consider. Can we control change? How do we determine when to manage change? When should we simply let change happen? These questions place leaders in a very delicate position. Humans tend to create routines for solving problems. The pace of change in our world has continued to accelerate for decades, and some individuals and organizations have struggled to keep up, such as with the iPhone, working online, or using Zoom for internet meetings.

A parent might decide to hire a tutor for a child who is struggling with their math classes. However, they would not hire a tutor to tell their child what outfits to wear to prom. Their belief might be that their child will grow out of it. In this book, we will present a perspective that strongly encourages a leader to be proactive. To do this, a leader must be proactive and have a solid understanding of change management.

Consider these five states in your change effort. I believe these five elements of change management will give you that jump-start:

- An overview of change management,
- Why and when change is necessary,
- Major barriers to change,
- A simple process for change,
- Tailored strategies for change.

A description of change management

Essentially, change management encompasses all the processes, tools, and techniques necessary for achieving positive business results. Keep in mind that these are all used by people in combination with other non-human elements.

Where and when change is needed

As I mentioned earlier, change occurs; you can't prevent it. However, some predictable events affect the organization and are seen as change. The following are some of the most significant.

New leaders at the top of an organization usually have their personality quirks that are often unknown and unpredictable. I have observed organizations with an annual turnover rate as high as 33% and as low as less than 1%. An organization that values diversity must frequently adapt to variations in values, attitudes, and beliefs. But we all adjust during these periods. If this leadership turnover remains high each year, other practices must be implemented to adapt to these changes.

Even a changing company goal or mission can be impactful. This can lead to changes in goals, standards, opportunities, separate tasks, orientation with new equipment and procedures, new regulatory policies and laws, realignment of functions, major mergers, or even shifts in the company's morality.

Significant Barriers To Change:

- Attendance at company meetings
- Protocol at meetings
- Focusing on every word of the leader when they are addressing the team
- Dress code
- Processes for presenting new ideas to the leadership
- Individual resistance to incorporating new practices or cultural norms
- Team members referring to how it was in their last organization (for better or worse)

Leaders who know their team well will observe how individual team members behave or the words they might share about the change initiative. That also includes their performance on the new equipment or their adherence to the safety procedures. Finally, are the leaders walking the talk?

A Simple Process For Change Is A Necessity.

Keep it simple, and the team will be able to pick it up quickly. There are many of these strategies. I like the Plan, Do, Act, Study (PDAS) approach used by many Total Quality advocates. Walter Shewhart introduced the PDAS cycle in the 1920s and is fundamental to Dr. W. E. Deming's organizational development and improvement.

The PDAS Procedure

- "**Plan**: Recognize an opportunity and **plan** a change.
- **Do:** Test the change. Carry out a small-scale study.
- **Act:** Review the test, analyze the results, and identify what you've learned.
- **Study:** Act based on what you learned in the study step."

<u>Total Quality Management and Plan Do Act Study –</u>

Google Search

Having a standard change approach or process can provide comfort to you and your team, but will there be automatic buy-in from all team members? Usually, there isn't complete agreement among team members at the start. The standard approach typically involves the leader and team members doing three things: preparing a plan, ensuring everyone understands the plan, and actively supervising the plan's implementation. Behaviorally, this means you need to stay aware of what is happening, support your team's needs, and communicate-communicate-communicate.

Remember the football team that knew the other team's play so well they preempted the other team in attempting to execute. These three measures are not easy, but the results will enhance the stock of your organization. And all will see you as a winner.

Tailored Strategies For Change.

Once again, this is a problem-solving event. Gather facts and make assumptions. Are subordinates being adequately trained to standard? The final strategy will be to measure the progress of change regularly. All too often, all parties can agree on a solution and later change their minds. It is also true that the answer may not meet expectations. Regular measurement will prevent major problems.

These three subjects (coaching, organizational assessment, and change management) are crucial for leaders at all levels to be effective. Master them, and you will quickly move into the successful ranks and find that you are much more proactive than you could imagine. Keep it up!

United States Army and Joint Staff Publications!

Chapter 11
The End and The Beginning*

"Only in the darkness can you see the stars."
Martin Luther King Jr.

In this book, we have explored the roles of leaders in organizations and the inherent tendency of organizations to exclude. Since the beginning, the most cliché phrase we often hear is "humans are social animals," which is true. Therefore, exclusion is an obstacle to the very thing that makes us human. Looking back at history, you'll see that early humans relied on one another, but their dependence wasn't necessarily for success. Instead, it was more about safety and survival. This impulsive tendency is deeply ingrained in the human brain, and it is the brain that reinforces it. Our decision-making is heavily influenced by fight-or-flight responses, which also impact our behavior.

The effort to create an inclusive environment is always deliberate and must be practiced for the benefit of everyone, the company, and especially the employees. Not only do our initiatives for inclusivity benefit us, but they also help build trust and engagement with our clients. The more inclusive the world becomes, the more likely logical reasoning will become more common. When that happens, humans will control the fight-or-flight response, and the world will be a much more peaceful and harmonious place. Without inclusion, we will quickly revert to our old habits, which aren't always helpful. We need to recognize that inclusion doesn't happen overnight. Instead, it is a step-by-step process that takes time. To understand this process, we have discussed the small details that serve as signposts, which readers will notice along the way as they explore this book.

There is a detailed discussion of the contributions made by the founding fathers of human relations. Some of the many names include Fredrick Taylor, Elton Mayo, and Douglas McGregor. We have also discussed the research they conducted and its impact on the art and science of inclusion. Research efforts, like the Hawthorn Experiment, explored the impact of the workforce environment.

Similarly, there is a discussion about Douglas McGregor's theories, known as Theories X and Y, which analyze different behaviors people have toward their work. We have also examined Abraham Maslow's Hierarchy of Needs, a frequently discussed model for human relations and management.

Numerous other factors contribute to the work environment, such as discrimination. These include discussions about the discrimination employees face or have faced in the past within their work environments, as well as the involvement of African Americans in race riots in Vietnam. There is also a detailed explanation of how discrimination and the lack of diversity and inclusion impact common goals. Additionally, when talking about diversity and inclusion, we see the difference between these two concepts, as they are often used interchangeably. In the same chapter, we discussed discrimination against African Americans in the military, how it leads to failure on the battlefield, and how this complex situation resulted in the formation of the DRRI. However, we can confidently say that the future will be more conducive to creating more inclusive work environments than ever before.

Right now, the world is fighting an uphill battle against the COVID-19 virus. Additionally, we are struggling with an economic crisis and repeated calls for social justice, which often clash with our ears. On the bright side, with high-speed internet and smart gadgets at our fingertips, we remain connected and sympathize with those who need to be heard and helped during these strange times. The best part is that influential figures have begun to voice their opinions and grievances, effectively utilizing available media platforms.

These influencers encompass a diverse range of individuals, including showbiz personalities, athletes, musicians, politicians, scientists, and academics. Meanwhile, ordinary people those not widely known are also gaining the courage to step forward and share their knowledge, skills, and whatever material benefits they can offer. If not to the world at large, then at least to those in their immediate surroundings. Even individuals who aren't the loudest advocates of inclusion are finding inspiration, which has motivated them to abandon their traditional thinking and start seeing the bigger picture. Businesses have already,

Started reaping the benefits of inclusion, such as a better workforce, new business opportunities, increased sales, and improved profitability. When it comes to workforce diversity, affirmative legal programs have played a significant role. Besides that, the social justice approach is gaining momentum, encouraging people to come together and invest in what is morally right. Both of these change philosophies are helpful to some extent. However, there are some obstacles companies often face, and one of them is the overall sum game. In the total sum game, it's believed that if one person gains, another must lose. Historically, under the guise of "White Privilege," white males have been favored, which is wrong; the right approach would be to move away from the big sum game.

However, another approach or model opens the way for effective human relations and human resources. That model is a strategic systems model. In many companies, diversity is present, but not many people value it, so they can't be as innovative and productive as they want to be. Therefore, specific behavior rules should be defined and implemented.

There should be a standard behavior all employees should follow. This will make it easier for them to interact with each other and work toward common goals. I have worked with leaders worldwide, and I strongly believe that to become a charismatic leader, you should prioritize inclusion as much as you prioritize your business growth. Through this book, I intend to give you an idea of what the new workplace could look like. I want it to be shared with everyone. A workplace should regularly help its people reach their potential. I truly believe that achieving this requires us to continuously grow from the initial stage of addressing human issues to that of advocacy, where we actively fight battles for the business. To reach that level, employees need to be valued by their superiors and colleagues. To perform effectively as a team, we must be willing to discuss people's problems and the solutions to those problems.

Initially, this book was meant to be just an account of my experiences in human relations. However, I have continually tried to inspire people to advocate for inclusion while I have been working—first as a race relations instructor and now as a consultant and executive coach—in their companies. I believe that this goal cannot be achieved solely through a few words on human relations or a few skills we have gained from reading about these topics.

These skills and desires should be combined with knowledge of human behavior. But that is not enough either. I have learned that forces are influencing us every day. In social sciences, I am searching for the knowledge and skills needed to shift from exclusion to inclusion. But how can I apply those skills to strategies? I believe that, just as our bodies rely on a process called homeostasis to maintain chemical balance, the world of human relations and behavior works similarly, to ensure we all get what we need physically and psychologically to be happy.and to reach our potential, we need individuals and organizations to combine science and art to fulfill it. The magic goes beyond numbers and law (civil and moral). I knew and worked for a leader who was loved and admired by members of the organization. They were a great team player who always thought and acted as though the team was more important. An ideal team player demonstrates an empathetic manner regularly. Effective with different people in the 3,000-person company, they were inspirational and motivating for all of us. Their most powerful weapon was their effective communication skills. Many noted how impactful they were as a listener rather than just a speaker. I knew their meeting schedule regularly included meetings with some team members at 5 A.M., then a full workday, and at 10 P.M., I would see them talking with the youngest employees in a parking lot.

There were no secrets. They knew who they were, worked hard to understand all their teammates, and were highly sensitive to the environment. Many units received awards, were promoted, and, more importantly, this unit consistently accomplished its mission. If we follow his course of action, we will stay ahead of our competition and lead our team to success more often than not. I have found that the medical model's use in solving people's issues requires more than just knowledge of "SCIENCE" and research/technology to create meaningful change. For it to truly be effective, especially amidst numerous diversity issues, it depends on how it is implemented, that is an "ART." "SCIENCE" encompasses all the knowledge you can acquire.

Chapter Summaries

Chapter 1: Leadership, Leadership, My Kingdom For Leadership

The passage explores the complex nature of leadership, emphasizing that effective leadership involves both the leader and the followers. It underscores the importance of building trust and guiding teams with a clear purpose, noting that leadership starts with small, intentional actions that set the tone for success. The text dispels common myths about leadership, such as the idea that it is innate or that the strongest or loudest people are natural leaders. Instead, it asserts that leadership is developed through ongoing learning, self-awareness, and adaptability. True leaders empower others, foster inclusive environments, and lead by example rather than through commands. They possess vision, empathy, and resilience, cultivating a culture of trust and collaboration to motivate their teams toward shared goals. Effective communication, prioritizing others' needs, and encouraging cooperation are identified as essential leadership skills. The passage concludes by emphasizing the importance of developing leadership abilities through training, setting clear goals, and understanding followers' needs, ultimately making a positive impact on the organization and beyond.

Chapter 2: The Leadership Mysteries Enigma

Effective leadership goes beyond just managing tasks; it involves empowering teams to reach their full potential. True leaders focus on developing people, building trust, encouraging creativity, and providing growth opportunities. They mentor, train, and inspire their teams, creating an environment where everyone can succeed. Clear communication is key; leaders need to listen and engage with their teams, avoiding poor communication habits that can hold back progress. Confidence and conviction are essential, as they help instill vision and empower the team. Adaptability is also important; leaders must embrace change and proactively handle challenges. Building strong relationships is crucial; leaders should support and understand their team members, fostering loyalty and a positive organizational culture. Effective task management involves recognizing team strengths and delegating tasks accordingly. Achieving meaningful results requires confidence and good decision-making skills, while poor leadership can lead to negative outcomes. Employee development is vital; leaders should invest in training and growth opportunities. Self-awareness is the foundation of good leadership; knowing one's strengths and weaknesses is essential. Tools like the Myers-Briggs Type Indicator and Gallup's StrengthsFinder 2.0 help leaders and teams understand their personalities and strengths, improving collaboration and performance. The virtues of the Ideal Team Player—humility, hunger, and smartness—are essential for effective teamwork. Strong communication, including listening, nonverbal cues, and empathy, is important for fostering a positive work environment. Leaders should provide ongoing development opportunities to support continuous growth and success.

Chapter 3: Developing Innovative and Inclusive Leadership Competencies

The passage highlights the importance of ongoing training and development for leaders to cultivate inclusive leadership and promote organizational success. It underscores various strategies, such as participating in educational opportunities, engaging in self-reflection, and seeking feedback, to deepen understanding of inclusion and diversity principles. Mentoring and coaching are essential for guiding leaders in adopting inclusive practices, while involvement in Employee Resource Groups (ERGs) offers direct insights into the diverse experiences of employees. Cross-cultural exposure, unconscious bias training, and cultural competence development are vital for broadening perspectives and improving inclusive communication. The passage also stresses the need for continual learning and growth, advocating for regular training to stay updated with industry trends and best practices. By embracing these strategies, organizations can empower leaders to build inclusive leadership skills and support diversity initiatives effectively. Additionally, the passage discusses key leadership qualities such as self-awareness, emotional intelligence, vision, strategic thinking, communication, decision-making, team building, adaptability, and resilience. It highlights the history and innovative programs of the Center for Creative Leadership, emphasizing the importance of visible commitment, humility, bias awareness, curiosity about others, cultural intelligence, and effective collaboration in leading an inclusive organization. Overall, the passage champions a well-structured professional development approach that enhances leadership capabilities, fosters employee engagement, and adapts to the changing business environment.

Chapter 4: Critical Thinking

The passage discusses the importance of critical thinking, emphasizing its role in making informed decisions and solving problems effectively. It starts by differentiating critical thinking from common sense, noting that while common sense is instinctive, critical thinking is a skill that must be learned, involving asking the right questions and challenging assumptions. The text highlights that critical thinking is about more than just finding answers; it involves assessing information and making well-informed choices. It also addresses biases and prejudices that can obstruct critical thinking and underscores the need for deliberate development of this skill. The passage details various tools of critical thinking, such as gathering information, observation, inference, rationalization, reflection, creation, classification, sequencing, comparison, cause-and-effect analysis, synthesis, evaluation, prediction, prioritization, and summarization. It stresses the importance of organizing and evaluating information by considering factors like relevance, authority, accuracy, and purpose. Additionally, the text explores how unconscious bias and macroaggressions can affect critical thinking and decision-making. It concludes by discussing the importance of reaching logical conclusions through different types of reasoning, including formal, symbolic, informal, and mathematical logic, and emphasizes evaluating major decisions by weighing their significance, impact, and potential costs. Overall, the passage underlines the vital role of critical thinking in navigating complex situations and making sound decisions.

Chapter 5: Role of I&I Professionals in Facilitating Change

The passage highlights the importance of Innovation and Inclusion (I&I) strategies in the corporate world, emphasizing that these approaches extend beyond traditional Diversity, Equity, and Inclusion (DEI) efforts. I&I strategies are vital for companies aiming to stay competitive and relevant in a diverse global market. The Institute for Diversity Certification (IDC) stresses that I&I professionals play a key role in creating workplaces where diverse perspectives are valued and all employees have equal opportunities to succeed. The chapter outlines the responsibilities of I&I professionals, including implementing policies that foster innovation and inclusion, creating roadmaps for organizational success, and maintaining a diverse and inclusive workforce. It also discusses the value of I&I professionals, who positively influence organizational success by promoting cohesion among a diverse workforce and creating a psychologically safe, barrier-free work environment. Key strategies for developing effective I&I initiatives include aligning I&I with organizational goals, building a comprehensive I&I framework, utilizing data and analytics, and ensuring ethical compliance. The chapter also explores change management, emphasizing the reasons for implementing change processes within organizations, the barriers to successful change, and the risks of poor change management. Ultimately, it underscores the importance of engaging and empowering I&I professionals, fostering cross-functional collaboration, and recognizing I&I professionals as change agents who overcome challenges, build inclusive cultures, and drive meaningful organizational change. Overall, the chapter underscores the vital role of I&I strategies in nurturing a culture of innovation and inclusion, which ultimately contributes to organizational success in a rapidly changing business environment.

Chapter 6: Understanding Power Dynamics and Privilege

The passage explores the widespread presence of power dynamics and privilege in different areas of life, including workplaces and community spaces. It notes that power imbalances are visible from a young age, such as in playgrounds and schools, where bullying is a form of abuse of power. As people grow older, these dynamics become more evident in professional environments. The text points out that privilege, whether based on gender, race, or class, has historically contributed to the oppression of certain groups. In workplaces, unchecked power disparities and privilege can stifle innovation, lower morale, and restrict opportunities for underrepresented groups. The passage stresses that understanding and addressing these dynamics is essential for building a productive and inclusive workplace. It recommends that organizations adopt inclusive policies, promote fair leadership development, and establish safe spaces for dialogue to empower employees from diverse backgrounds. Doing so can foster a culture of respect and shared responsibility, leading to long-term success. The passage also details different types of power in the workplace, such as positional, personal, and social capital. It discusses how power imbalances negatively affect decision-making, workplace culture, and employee engagement. Lastly, it offers suggestions for managing power dynamics, including offering training on innovation and inclusion, creating structured hiring and promotion processes, setting up mentorship programs, supporting employee resource groups, promoting open communication, and providing flexible work options. Overall, the passage underscores the importance of recognizing and addressing power dynamics and privilege to build a fairer and more successful workplace.

Chapter 7: Engaging Employee Resource Groups (ERGs) and Allies

Employee Resource Groups (ERGs), also called Affinity Groups or Employee Networks, are voluntary, employee-led groups that unite individuals sharing common backgrounds, experiences, or identities. ERGs offer a platform for employees to connect, support each other, and promote inclusivity within the organization. The process of implementing ERGs generally includes defining purpose and scope, gaining support and leadership, recruiting members, setting governance and structure, and planning and executing programs and activities. Allies are individuals who actively support and advocate for members of marginalized or underrepresented groups, even if they do not belong to those groups. Allies leverage their privilege and influence to foster inclusive environments and challenge biases and discrimination. The stages of engaging allies typically involve education and awareness, creating an ally network, encouraging dialogue and listening, amplifying marginalized voices, and promoting ongoing learning and growth. By following these steps for ERGs and engaging allies, organizations can create a more inclusive and supportive environment where Inclusion & Innovation (I&I) initiatives integrate into all areas of the organization, leading to better employee engagement, retention, and overall success. This chapter offers a complete guide to developing inclusive leadership skills and involving ERGs and allies to advance Inclusion and Innovation (I&I) within organizations. It highlights the vital role of ERGs in building community and fostering belonging and provides guidance for establishing and supporting ERGs as platforms for networking, advocacy, and driving I&I efforts. Implementing these steps for ERGs and engaging allies helps organizations cultivate a more inclusive, supportive culture where I&I initiatives permeate every aspect, resulting in improved employee commitment, retention, and overall organizational achievement.

Chapter 8: Culture

Chapter 8 examines the vital role of organizational culture in shaping the workplace environment and employee experiences. It discusses the challenges employees face, including increased health-related issues, workplace violence, and burnout, which have worsened due to the COVID-19 pandemic. The chapter stresses that a healthy, supportive culture is key to long-term success because it impacts motivation, well-being, and a sense of belonging.

Organizational culture, described as the unwritten social framework of an institution, permanently influences attitudes and behaviors. The Defense Equal Opportunity Management Institute (DEOMI) highlights the importance of recognizing and considering culture when developing strategies to build an inclusive organization. Edgar Schein's categories of culture—macro-cultures, organizational cultures, subcultures, and micro-cultures—are discussed, along with the difference between managerial and corporate culture. The chapter also covers how values and cultural beliefs develop, emphasizing that culture is learned and passed down through generations. Cultural intelligence (CQ) is presented as a critical skill for leaders to effectively manage multicultural environments. The four CQ capabilities—CQ Drive, CQ Knowledge, CQ Strategy, and CQ Action—are outlined as a framework to help leaders improve their cultural intelligence and foster inclusive workplaces. Overall, the chapter stresses the importance of investing in a positive organizational culture to create an environment where employees feel heard, valued, and empowered to succeed.

Chapter 9: VUCA - The Nature of Our World

Chapter 9 examines the concept of VUCA, an acronym for Volatility, Uncertainty, Complexity, and Ambiguity, which describes the difficult and unpredictable nature of today's global economic and political environment. The chapter starts by discussing the impact of new tariffs imposed by the United States, leading to significant market losses and international concern. It then explains the definitions and effects of VUCA, emphasizing how leaders across industries must adapt quickly, make decisions with incomplete information, and maintain stability in unstable situations. The chapter details the four elements of VUCA: volatility, marked by rapid and intense changes; uncertainty, where cause-and-effect relationships are unclear; complexity, involving interconnected problems and hidden layers; and ambiguity, characterized by a lack of clarity and the potential for misinterpretation. It stresses the importance of understanding

VUCA to improve strategic skills and achieve better outcomes. The chapter also covers the historical background of VUCA, how it applies to various situations, and the necessity for leaders to use the VUCA framework to assess risks and create mitigation plans. It explores the links between the four components and includes thought exercises to identify VUCA in different scenarios. The chapter concludes by showing how VUCA helps people anticipate surprises and outcomes, develop mitigation and response strategies, and navigate today's fast-changing corporate landscape. Overall, Chapter 9 highlights the role of VUCA in modern leadership, strategy, and survival, providing valuable insights on how leaders can effectively manage and succeed in a VUCA world.

Chapter 10: Leadership and Management Strategies

Chapter 10 highlights the importance of leadership and management strategies in a VUCA (Volatility, Uncertainty, Complexity, Ambiguity) business environment. It starts by sharing the author's personal experiences and strategies for reducing anxiety when beginning a new job, such as conducting reconnaissance to familiarize oneself with the new setting. The chapter then explains various ways to gain knowledge about a new job, including asking the previous role holder, learning on the job, and letting experience guide you. The author promotes a systematic approach and emphasizes the benefits of executive coaching, organizational assessments, and change management training for new executives, especially at the senior level. It outlines a detailed agency coaching program, stressing the importance of coaching in speeding up the development and effectiveness of high-potential employees. The chapter also discusses the role of organizational assessments in understanding the climate and dynamics of a new organization, along with the importance of change management in controlling and adapting to change. It concludes by stressing that continuous learning and development are essential for leaders to navigate the complexities of a VUCA environment effectively. Overall, Chapter 10 provides a comprehensive guide for new leaders to develop their skills, understand their organization, and implement strategies for success in a rapidly changing business landscape.

Leadership And Management Strategies

Generally, you have a few methods to acquire the knowledge you need to perform your job quickly. I believe the following approach will help you get there. An executive coach can start by developing your coaching philosophy and guidance. Coaching is an intensive, one-on-one professional relationship designed to accelerate the growth and effectiveness of high-potential individuals within the agency.

An Organizational Climate Assessment Outline is the quintessential process to learn what your organization is all about. I have provided a step-by-step approach to achieving this objective.

1. The pre-preparation stages
2. Preparing organization members for an upcoming survey
3. Conducting the Survey
4. Interpreting the data
5. Outlining for briefings
6. Conducting the leadership briefings
7. Extending briefing to the organization members
8. Conducting Hot Wash session with the assessment team

Change is a constant, and we must understand how to influence it. That ability starts with a clear and focused understanding. To accomplish this, I have reduced it to three major areas of interest and focus: Understanding change management, identifying the need for change, and the efforts to maintain and improve the change elements put in place. Consider these five stages in your change effort. I believe these five elements of change management will give you that jump-start:

1. An overview of change management
2. Why and when change is necessary
3. Major barriers to change
4. A simple process for change
5. Tailored strategies for change.

These three subjects (coaching, organizational assessment, and change management) are crucial for leaders at all levels to be effective. Master them, and you will quickly move into the successful ranks and find that you are much more proactive than you could imagine. Keep it up!

We reach a point in this book where I believe we are ready to take the next step. I believe an introduction to Janus, the God of many things. I choose to use this Roman God to express my sentiments and best wishes for you:

The God of Gates, Doors, and Transitions:
History of the Roman God Janus

In ancient Roman religion and mythology, Janus was considered the god of gates and doors.... the ancient Romans had a specific god who held the key, so to speak, to the metaphorical doors or gateways between what was and what is to come—the liminal space of transitioning out of one period of time and into something new...

Who Is JanUS?

"In Roman mythology, Janus was the god of doors, gates, and transitions. Janus represented the middle ground between the dualities of concrete and abstract, such as life/death, beginning/end, youth/adulthood, rural/urban, war/peace, and barbarism/civilization.

According to Roman mythology, Janus was present at the beginning of the world. As the god of gates, Janus guarded the gates of heaven and <u>held access</u> to heaven and other gods. For this reason, Janus was often invoked first in ancient Roman religious ceremonies, and during public sacrifices, offerings were given to Janus *before any other deity. In fact, there is evidence that Janus was worshipped long before many of the other Roman gods, dating all the way back to the time of Romulus (the founder and first ruler of Rome).*

And if you've ever wondered how the month of January got its name, you have Janus to thank. As the Roman god of beginnings and transitions, Janus is the namesake of January, the first month of a new year.

Why Does Janus Have 2 Faces?

What is unusual about the god Janus is his iconic image. As the god of transitions and dualities, Janus is portrayed with two faces — one facing the past and one facing the future. He also holds a key in his right hand, which symbolizes his protection of doors, gates, thresholds, and other separations or openings between spaces. In ancient Rome, the symbol of the key also signified that a traveler has come to find safe harbor or trade goods in peace.

andersOnlock.com

I sincerely pray that this book will allow you to begin anew.

*Change always starts with the image of the person in the mirror

Appendix A
END NOTES

Appendix A
END NOTES

Chapter 1

1. Goleman, Daniel in his popular book, Emotional Intelligence 2.0,
2. Kevin Kelley, 2009
3. Michael Korda described the reaction in his book *Ike: An American Hero*: "Patton

Chapter 2

1. 1944 as the Briggs Myers Type Indicator was later renamed Myers-Briggs Type Indicator in 1956.
2. Gallup's StrengthsFinder 2.0 (initially published in 2007).
3. Patrick Lencioni's book (2016) *The Ideal Team Player: How to Recognize and Cultivate the Three Essential Virtues*
4. ***Socrates.***

Chapter 3

1. The Top 7 Change Management Models for Effective Organizational Change - Culture Partners
2. Carnegie, D. (1936). How to Win Friends and Influence People. Simon & Schuster.
3. Citation: Goleman, D. (1995). Emotional Intelligence. Bantam Books.
4. Heifetz, R., & Linsky, M. (2002). Leadership on the Line. Harvard Business Review Press.
5. Kahneman, D. (2011). Thinking, Fast and Slow. Farrar, Straus and Giroux.

6. Kotter's Eight-Step Process for Leading Change Citation: Kotter, J.P. (1996). Leading Change. Harvard Business Review Press.
7. [Kotter's 8 Step Change Model in Six Sigma: A Comprehensive Guide to Successful Organizational Change - SixSigma.us](#)
8. Lencioni, P. (2002). The Five Dysfunctions of a Team. Jossey-Bass.
9. Simon Sinek
10. [The Top 7 Change Management Models for Effective Organizational Change - Culture Partners](#)
11. [Why Inclusive Leaders Are Good for Organizations, and How to Become One](#)

Chapter 4

1. *Aristotle*
2. Cerritos College medical courses. SOAP: S. (subject) O. (objective) A. (assessment) P. (plan). 1 9 7 1 .

Chapter 5

1. Daryl Conner
2. DEI. Institute for Diversity Certification (IDC). 2024

Chapter 6

1. Brouard, P. (2022). Privilege and power in the workplace - Digital Frontiers Institute. Digital Frontiers Institute. https://digitalfrontiersinstitute.org/privilege-and-power-in-the-workplace/
2. Marc Benioff Bio - Salesforce.com US. (n.d.). Salesforce. Retrieved June 27, 2024, from https://www.salesforce.com/company/marc-benioff-bio/
3. **Maxwell, John I. *The 21 Irrefutable Laws of Leadership: Follow Them and People Will Follow You. Jun 2022.***

4. Power Dynamics in Research | Definition, Examples & Awareness - ATLAS.ti. (2024). ATLAS.Ti. https://atlasti.com/guides/qualitative-research-guide-part-1/power-dynamics

Chapter 7

1. Bolton Sr.. José. Ph.D. *Innovation by Design*. 2025.

Chapter 8

1. CGLI. *Diversity Wheel. Cultural Competence Learning Institute.* Retrieved from: https://community.astc.org/ccli/resources-for-action/group-activities/diversity-wheel
2. Changingminds.org. *Values Development*. Retrieved from: http://changingminds.org/explanations/values/values_development.htm
3. Charlton, James I., *'Culture(s) and Belief Systems', Nothing About Us Without Us: Disability Oppression and Empowerment* (Oakland, CA, 1998; online edn, California Scholarship Online, May 24, 2012), https://doi.org/10.1525/california/9780520207950.003.0004
4. Correia, A. 2017. *The "Yers" Millennials from a Morris Massey Perspective*. ISFSI. Retrieved from: https://www.isfsi.org/blog/the-yers-millenials-from-a-morris-massey-perspective
5. Ebrary.net. *Organizational Culture*. Retrieved from: https://ebrary.net/3030/management/organizational_culture
6. Groysberg, B., Lee, J., Price, J., & Cheng, Y. *The Leader's Guide to Corporate Culture: How to Manage the Eight Critical Elements of Organizational Life,* 2018. Harvard Business Review. Retrieved from: https://hbr.org/2018/01/the-leaders-guide-to-corporate-culture
7. Gruenert and Whitaker, 2017, pp. 3–4.
8. Harrison, R. (1972). *Understanding your organization's character*. Harvard Business Review, 50 (3), 119–128.
9. Jaspers, E. (2016). Values. Oxford Bibliographies in Sociology Doi: https://doi.org/10.1093/OBO/9780199756384-0182

10. Loden, M. (1995). *Implementing Diversity: Best Practices for Making Diversity Work in Your Organization* McGraw-Hill Education.
11. Marshak, R. J. (2006) *Covert processes at work* San Francisco: Berrett-Koehler
12. McIntosh, P. (1989). *White Privilege: Unpacking the Invisible Knapsack* Peace and freedom Retrieved from: https://psychology.umbc.edu/wp-content/uploads/sites/57/2016/10/White-Privilege_McIntosh-1989.pdf
13. Ramsay, K. 2022. Morris Massey's *Stages of Values Development. Achology.* Retrieved from: https://achology.com/morris-masseys-stages-of-values-development/
14. Schein, E.H. (2010) *Organizational Culture and Leadership (4th Edition)* Josey-Bass: Wiley, pp. 13
15. Schein, E.H. (2010) *Organizational Culture and Leadership (4th Edition)* Josey-Bass: Wiley.
16. The Defense Equal Opportunity Management Institute (DEOMI)
17. Usó-Doménech, J.L., and Nescolarde-Selva, J. What are belief systems? Found Sci 21, 147–152 (2016). https://doi.org/10.1007/s10699-015-9409-z
18. Weller, S.C. (2005). *Cultural Consensus Model.* Encyclopedia of Social Measurement Editor: Kempf-Leonard K. Elsevier.
19. *What is culture?* Center for Advanced Research on Language Acquisition CARLA. Retrieved from: https://carla.umn.edu/culture/definitions.html
20. Wilderom, C. P. M., Glunk, U., & Maslowski, R. (2000). *Organizational culture as a predictor of organizational performance* In N. M. Ashkanasy, C. P. M. Wilderom, and M. F. Peterson (Eds.), Handbook of Organizational Culture and Climate Thousand Oaks, CA: Sage, pp. 193–209.

Chapter 9

1. (PDF) VUCA Concept and Leadership (researchgate.net)
2. Allen, C.D. and Coates, B.E. (2009). The engagement of military voice. *Parameters: US Army War College*, 39(4), 73–87.

3. Barber, Herbert F. *"Developing Strategic Leadership: The US Army War College Experience." Journal of Management Development* 11, no. 6 (1992): 4-12
4. Bennett, N. and Lemoine, G.J. (2014). *What a difference a word makes: Understanding threats to performance in a VUCA world. Business Horizons* 57, 311–317.
5. Bennis, W., & Nanus, B. *(Leaders: The Strategies For Taking Charge)*. 1985.
6. Çiçeklioğlu, Hüseyin VUCA Concept and Leadership. on November 29 2020.
7. Effective Decision-Making in a VUCA Environment
8. Goldsmith, Marshall, and Teiter, Mark. *What Got You Here Won't Get You There: How Successful People Become Even More Successful.* January 9, 2007.
9. Heidrick & Struggles Study - 40% Executives Gone in 18 Months
10. Kinsinger, P. and Walch, K. (2012). *Living and leading in a VUCA world.* Thunderbird University, Retrieved, Phoenix.
11. Nelson Mandela
12. Nelson, Bob. And Economy, Peter. *Managing For Dummies.* 2003
13. Rajesh, M., Ekambaram, K., Rakesh, S., & Kumar, A. (2019)
14. Shaffer, L.S. and Zalewski, J.M. (2011). *Career advising in a VUCA environment.* NACADA Journal, 31(1), 64–74.
15. Sharma, P. (2015). *Is your workforce VUCA-ready?* https://trogonsoftteamwise.word press.com/ (Date of Access: 10.06.2020).

Chapter 10

1. (20) 7 Leadership Lessons from a Battle of the Bulge Veteran, 101st Airborne Division Paratrooper | LinkedIn
2. 7 Leadership Lessons from a Battle of the Bulge Veteran, 101st Airborne Division Paratrooper | LinkedIn

3. Goldsmith, Marshall, and Teiter, Mark. *What Got You Here Won't Get You There: How Successful People Become Even More Successful.* January 9, 2007.
4. Heidrick & Struggles Study - 40% Executives Gone in 18 Months
5. Total Quality Management and Plan Do Act Study – Google Search
6. United States Army and Joint Staff Publications
7. What is Leadership? A ResourcefulManager guide

Frequently Utilized Websites

www.wikkipedia.org

www.eeoc.gov

www.dol.gov

www.ssa.gov

www.census.gov

www.youtube.com

www.hbr.org

www.diversityinc.com

www.shrm.org

www.ehow.com

www.census.gov

www.DEOMI.org

1. Total Quality Management and Plan-Do-Act-Study - Google Search
2. pdsacycledebedits.pdf
3. What Is QAPI? Facility Guide and FAQ | IntelyCare

www.ingramcontent.com/pod-product-compliance
Lightning Source LLC
Chambersburg PA
CBHW050906160426
43194CB00011B/2311